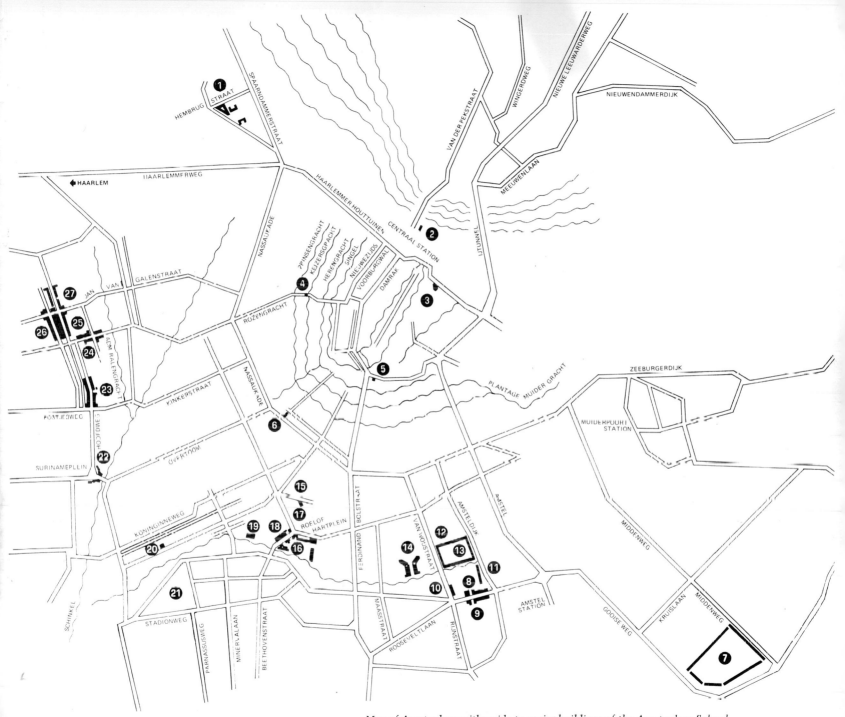

Map of Amsterdam with guide to major buildings of the Amsterdam School.
Based on material provided by the Stedelijk Museum, Amsterdam. See key, overleaf

KEY TO MAP

1. Michel de Klerk, three housing blocks on the Spaarndammerplantsoen: Oostzaanstraat 2–6 / Spaarndammerplantsoen 14–36, 1913–15, for K. Hille; Zaanstraat 48–49 / Spaarndammerplantsoen 11–31 / Wormerveerstraat 17–19, 1914–16, for Eigen Haard; Zaanstraat 54–64 / Hembrugstraat 57–77 / Oostzaanstraat 1–21, 1917–21, for Eigen Haard

2. G. F. la Croix, shipping agency's office, De Ruyterkade, 1919

3. J. M. van der Mey, in collaboration with Michel de Klerk and Piet Kramer, Scheepvaarthuis, Prins Hendrikkade / Binnenkant / Buiten Bantammerstraat, 1912–16

4. Piet Kramer, bridge over the Keizersgracht, on Raadhuisstraat, 1922

5. J. Gidding, interior design of entrance of Tuschinski Theater, Reguliersbreestraat 26–28, 1920–21

6. Piet Kramer and J. Polet, bridge over Singelgracht, on Leidseplein, 1925

7. D. Greiner, J. B. van Loghem, J. Gratama, and others, Betondorp, situated between the streets Duivendrechtselaan, Onderlangs, Middenweg, and Zaaiersweg, 1921–26

8. Michel de Klerk, housing blocks on Vrijheidslaan 10–48 / Kromme Mijdrechtstraat 1–5 / Meerhuizenplein 7–11, 34–38 / Kromme Mijdrechtstraat 2–4 / Vrijheidslaan 50–54, 1921–22

9. Piet Kramer, housing blocks on Vrijheidslaan 9–43 / Kromme Mijdrechtstraat 11–15, 6–10 / Vrijheidslaan 45–47, 1921–22

10. J. Boterenbrood, housing blocks on Rijnstraat 37–57, 30a–54 / IJselstraat 1–9, 2–8 / Berkelstraat 21–23, 1923–25

11. M. Kropholler, housing block on Amstelkade 3–5 / Holendrechtstraat 1–47 / Uithoornstraat 6, 1922

12. J. C. van Epen, housing blocks in an area bounded by Diamantstraat, Jozef Israelskade, Amsteldijk, and Saffierstraat, 1922

13. A. J. Westerman, public baths, Diamantstraat, 1925

14. Michel de Klerk and Piet Kramer, housing blocks for De Dageraad on P. L. Takstraat 1–29, 2–30 / Burg. Tellegenstraat 14–36, 38–60 / Willem Pastoorsstraat 26–36 / Talmastraat 2–12 / Th. Schwartzestraat 1–19 / Th. Schwartzeplein 1–33 / H. Ronnerstraat 2–18 / H. Ronnerplein 2–34, 1919–21

15. Michel de Klerk, housing block on N. Maesstraat 32–34 / J. Vermeerplein 34 / G. Metsustraat 22–34, 1911–12

16. J. C. van Epen, housing blocks on Hobbemakade / Reinier Vinkeleskade / Harmoniehof, 1920–22

17. J. Boterenbrood, Huize Lydia, Roelof Hartplein 2, 1925

18. J. F. Staal, housing blocks on J. M. Coenenstraat / Barth. Ruloffstraat / Bronckhorststraat, 1922

19. Piet Kramer, housing block on Heinzestraat 13–23, 1921

20. Piet Kramer, Het Zwarte Huis (The Black House), Okeghemstraat 25–27, 1921

21. Housing blocks designed by different architects under supervision of J. Gratama, 1921–c. 1930

22. J. Roodenburgh, housing blocks on Hoofdweg 8–27 / Surinameplein 2–24 / Surinamestraat 2–40 / Baarsjesweg 313 / Sloterkade 1–9 / Surinamestraat 1–11 / Surinameplein 1–27, 1928

23. Piet Kramer, housing blocks on Van Spilbergenstraat 4 / Postjesweg 98–110 / Hoofdweg 136–232, 43–241 / Davisstraat 47–59, 48–56 / Hudsonstraat 1–7, 37–51 / Willem Schoutenstraat 31–35 / Van Spilbergenstraat 92–96, 1923–25

24. J. F. Staal, housing blocks on Admiralengracht 212–21, 223–29 / J. Evertsenstraat 43–131, 52–140 / Marco Polostraat 224–32, 219–25 / John Franklinstraat 2–8, 1–7 / Vespuccistraat 29–45, 26–42 / Barth. Diazstraat 26–30, 32–38, 1925

25. H. Th. Wijdeveld, housing blocks on Hoofdweg 308–82, 312–411 / Jan van Galenstraat 291–93, 184–88, 1925–27

26. M. Kropholler, housing blocks on Ortheliusstraat 203–93, 200–290 / Jan van Galenstraat 190–204, 295–309, 1925–26

27. J. M. van der Mey, housing blocks on Hoofdweg 413–91, 384–456 / Jan van Galenstraat 172–78, 283–89 / Hondiusstraat 9–10 / Erasmusgracht 11–15, 1926

THE AMSTERDAM SCHOOL
DUTCH EXPRESSIONIST ARCHITECTURE, 1915-1930

Wim de Wit, GENERAL EDITOR

COOPER-HEWITT MUSEUM
The Smithsonian Institution's National Museum of Design,
New York

The MIT Press
Cambridge, Massachusetts
London, England

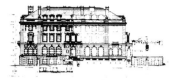

Cooper-Hewitt Museum
The Smithsonian Institution's National Museum of Design
2 East 91st Street, New York, N.Y. 10128

Publication Coördinator: Lucy Fellowes
Editor: Lory Frankel

150 Fifth Avenue, New York, N.Y. 10011

Managing Editor: Clive Giboire
Creative Director: Arnold Skolnick
Editorial Assistant: Suzanne Gagné
Art Associate: Nancy Crompton
Production: Karen Fox
Typography: Larry Lorber, Ultracomp

The MIT Press
28 Carleton Street, Cambridge, Massachusetts 02142

Library of Congress Cataloging in Publication Data
Main entry under title:
The Amsterdam school.
    Bibliography: p.
    Includes index.
    1. Amsterdamse school (Architecture)—Addresses,
essays, lectures. 2. Expressionism (Art)—Influence—
Addresses, essays, lectures. 3. Architecture, Modern—
20th century—Netherlands—Addresses, essays, lectures.
4. Klerk, Michel de, 1884-1923—Addresses, essays,
lectures. I. Wit, Wim de.
NA1148.5.A4A47   1983   720'.9492'3   83-72390
ISBN 0-910503-21-4 (paper)
ISBN 0-262-04074-3 (cloth)

10 9 8 7 6 5 4 3 2 1

Printed and bound in the United States

CONTENTS

ACKNOWLEDGMENTS

The organization of an exhibition, especially one with materials from abroad, is impossible without the help and support of a large number of people. I would like to express my grateful appreciation to all those who have contributed to the realization of "The Amsterdam School: Dutch Expressionist Architecture, 1915-1930."

I am most thankful to Dick van Woerkom, director of the Nederlands Documentatiecentrum voor de Bouwkunst in Amsterdam, who generously agreed to lend a large number of rich and important architectural materials for this purpose. Without his support this exhibition would not have taken place. Mariet Willinge, assistant director, and the rest of the NDB staff have also given time and careful attention to the numerous details involved in such a transatlantic undertaking. Other crucial support for the exhibition came in the form of loans from Arthur Staal, Nicolai Huisman Langhout architecten, the Stedelijk Museum, Gemeentelijke Archiefdienst, and Stichting Architectuurmuseum, all of Amsterdam. I am indebted to the directors and staffs of these institutions for their cooperation in every respect.

In addition, the Rijksdienst voor de Monumentenzorg in Zeist graciously offered its services in making many photographs available for the catalogue.

Of all the individuals who assisted me in preparing this exhibition, Helen Searing has been outstanding in every way. She not only made initial contacts with the Cooper-Hewitt Museum, but continued to give freely of her profound knowledge and wide experience throughout the organization process. In the difficult task of selecting and classifying the materials in the exhibition, I was fortunate to have the aid and thoughtful advice of Maristella Casciato. I am very much obliged to her for all the time she devoted to this demanding work. The same is true of Richard Pommer, who gave me invaluable advice with regard to this book. Frans van Burkom amiably allowed the use of one of his essays as a basis for the discussion of Amsterdam School furniture and interior designs contained in the present catalogue. I would also like to extend my thanks to Ellinoor Bergvelt and Michiel Jonker, who helped me with many practical problems and offered advice and insights to the Dutch contributors to the catalogue. All the authors richly deserve my respect and thanks for their enlightening essays. My thanks, as well, to Charlotte I. Loeb, Sandro Marpillero, Carolina Hatton, and Piera Watkins, who ably translated them. For the production of the publication, I was greatly aided by the intelligent editing, patience, and good humor of Lory Frankel; Arnold Skolnick and Clive Giboire of the design office Imago did a wonderful job in designing the book.

We are pleased that MIT Press has joined us in this venture; the enthusiasm and flexibility of Roger Conover greatly contributed to the publication of this book.

I want to express my gratitude to my director and colleagues at the Chicago Historical Society, who showed so much interest in the exhibition and never complained when I had to go to New York for it.

Lisa Taylor, director of the Cooper-Hewitt Museum, merits my most sincere thanks. Out of her enthusiastic admiration for the Amsterdam School, she gave me the opportunity to make this exhibition at her museum. Mrs. Taylor credits her introduction to these architects to Norbert Messler. Without the inspired dedication of the Cooper-Hewitt staff, particularly that of exhibition coordinators Lucy Fellowes and Dorothy Globus, designer Robin Parkinson, and registrar Cordelia Rose, this exhibition could not have been realized. The contributions of the Friends of the Cooper-Hewitt Museum also greatly aided this undertaking.

KLM Royal Dutch Airlines graciously provided transportation for the curator and couriers.

Wim de Wit

FOREWORD

IRONICALLY, in spite of radical technological and social changes, our concerns as we face a new millennium are not altogether different from those prevalent at the turn of the century. At that time, the Machine was viewed as a savior. It was to lead the way to a new age, in which the great masses of people no longer had to struggle for survival. While technology has indeed increased our material comforts, it has created a world in which, too often, the human dimension is overlooked. This has made a vacuum in our lives that cries to be filled. We look to contemporary architecture, among the other arts, to address this need.

Yet, in recent years, architects have tended to look back rather than ahead. Drawing upon traditional sources for inspiration is perfectly valid, as long as this is viewed as a point of departure. Today, architecture has a greater variety of means at its disposal than ever before with which to create technically excellent, functional, humanistic, and beautiful building forms. The opportunity to forge a new and brilliant architectural sensibility expressive of our age is within our grasp. To do so, architecture, which is preeminently a utilitarian art, must be able to solve current problems in contemporary ways.

Whether we like the end results or not, we cannot deny that the twentieth century has been one of the most exciting and productive epochs in architectural history. If modern architecture has failed us, as many seem to think, it is important to discover why. The early years, which were particularly vital and creative, shaped subsequent decades. A plethora of different movements sprang up, each with its own solutions. Studying their ideals, influences, sources, development, and contributions is not only fascinating but also instructive.

Because an awareness of expressionism in its many manifestations is critical to our understanding of modern architecture, it is surprising that so little attention has been devoted to the work of the prominent Dutch expressionist architects, led by Michel de Klerk, who formed what has become known as the Amsterdam School. Influential for over a dozen years beginning with World War I, the group left an aesthetic imprint that is still strongly visible in Amsterdam, one which provides an eloquent testimony to its achievements.

The activities of the Amsterdam School coincided with those of De Stijl. However, there were significant differences in the approach of each group. While De Stijl largely divorced itself from politics, the Amsterdam School came to fruition within a political context; its most successful projects were municipal commissions, notably public housing for low-income workers. Whereas De Stijl defined a purist aesthetic shared by the International Style that followed, the Amsterdam School favored a mode of individual expression whose applications were as diverse as its architects.

Although the Cooper-Hewitt has explored the roots of modernism before, we are especially proud to be the first museum outside the Netherlands to analyze the unique and inspiring accomplishments of De Klerk and the Amsterdam School. In doing so, we hope that this long-overlooked highpoint of expressionism will finally be accorded international recognition. We are deeply grateful to Wim de Wit and the individuals and institutions acknowledged elsewhere in this book for enabling us to realize this exciting undertaking, which was kindly supported by the Friends of the Cooper-Hewitt Museum.

Lisa Taylor
Director
Cooper-Hewitt Museum

INTRODUCTION

IT WAS not until the end of the 1960s that the Amsterdam School—a group of Dutch expressionist architects and designers active between about 1915 and 1930—first became a subject of serious research. At that time, expressionism in architecture emerged as a focus of scholarly concern. However, the specific meaning of this term needs to be explored with regard to the Amsterdam School, whose members never used it themselves. A definition can be achieved through a consideration of the group's own attitude toward their work and, in particular, toward the process of designing, which they regarded as an individual struggle with the demands of construction and materials in order to attain the ideal image that each artist saw deep within himself.

Between 1930 and 1965, functionalist theories in architecture prevailed, not only among architects but also among those who studied the history of architecture. Scarcely anyone was interested in the Amsterdam School, whose orientation was decidedly not functionalist, what little attention was accorded the group often amounted to a negative judgment of its products as well as its aims. The only exception to this viewpoint was offered by Henry-Russell Hitchcock in *Architecture: Nineteenth and Twentieth Centuries*, first published in 1958. Two years later, in his *Theory and Design in the First Machine Age*, Reyner Banham offered a positive discussion of the Amsterdam School, but he still considered it a minor byway in the development toward functionalism. He pronounced the Amsterdam School to be a "late outcropping" of attitudes dating from before the First World War that became "increasingly unacceptable on formal grounds after 1918."

Having figured as a part of these and other studies, such as Dennis Sharp's *Modern Architecture and Expressionism* (1966) and Giovanni Fanelli's *Architettura Moderna in Olanda 1900–1940* (1968), around 1970 the Amsterdam School became a subject in its own right with the appearance of two American dissertations. In "Michel de Klerk (1884–1923): An Architect of the Amsterdam School," Suzanne Frank established De Klerk's position as leader of the movement; Helen Searing's "Housing in Holland and the Amsterdam School" proved to be a seminal discussion of the Amsterdam School's deep involvement with public housing.

Even in the Netherlands, the first serious attempt to assess the Amsterdam School was not made until 1975. As part of a series of exhibitions on Dutch architecture in the first half of the twentieth century, the Stedelijk Museum in Amsterdam organized an exhibition devoted to the Amsterdam School. While of tremendous importance, the catalogue betrays the fact that it was the first scholarly study of the Amsterdam School to appear in the Netherlands: it tried to give a historical survey of the group in relation to the period in which it was active but did not offer an analysis of sources and backgrounds. The exhibition also had its

Michel de Klerk. Self-portrait, 1915. Crayon. Collection Nederlands Documentatiecentrum voor de Bouwkunst (NDB), Amsterdam

Michel de Klerk and Piet Kramer. Housing block on Pieter Lodewijk Takstraat and Burgemeester Tellegenstraat, Amsterdam, for De Dageraad, 1919–21

limitations, insofar as it took a formal-
ist approach to the Amsterdam School's
work and did not demonstrate how the
group as a whole functioned—that is,
how the architects influenced one
another and benefited from the political
circumstances of the time.

In the intervening years, interest in
the Amsterdam School has continued to
grow, providing impetus for a new
exhibition as well as for the publication
of recent research. In spite of the early
studies devoted to the school in such
countries as the United States and Italy,
a complete study in book form has
never been published nor has an exhibition been organized outside the Netherlands. The many people outside the
Netherlands who are still unacquainted
with the architecture and designs of the
Amsterdam School will benefit by this
chance to study its work. Besides offering the background and history of the
school, this book and exhibition re-
examine its legacy, in both theory and
practice, which is relevant to all fields
of design today. As artists and architects
seek to endow traditional decorative
forms with meaning, the Amsterdam
School presents a rich, expressive
language worthy of study, as well as
principles that once again seem appli-
cable. Equally important is the opportunity afforded here to consider the
results in good housing that were
achieved through the collaboration of
these architects with their city's government.

The hundredth anniversary of the
birth of Michel de Klerk, the most im-

J. M. van der Mey, in collaboration with Michel de Klerk and Piet Kramer. Scheepvaarthuis, on Prins Hendrikkade and Binnenkant, Amsterdam, 1912–16. Photograph, Collection NDB, Amsterdam. Opposite: *Detail of entrance*

14

Piet Kramer. Bridge over Singelgracht, on Leidseplein, Amsterdam, 1925. Sculpture by J. Polet

portant and prolific member of the school, provides a timely occasion to fill this lacuna and to celebrate his achievements. In his time, De Klerk was the most acclaimed architect of the Amsterdam School, and his predominance within the group is still accepted today. In his collaboration with Piet Kramer and Johan van der Mey on the Scheepvaarthuis (Shipping Building) in Amsterdam from 1912 to 1916, De Klerk was primarily responsible for establishing the path along which his colleagues, and later others, were to follow. With the completion of his three housing blocks at the Spaarndammerplantsoen (1913–21), the fame of the Amsterdam School was assured: architects from the world over came to see these landmark structures.

In the context of the book and the accompanying exhibition, De Klerk's architecture is seen to exemplify the style of the Amsterdam School as a whole. However, he was no isolated genius inventing his own style, nor did he work in a vacuum, creating masterpieces without any contact with the world around him. There was a lively give and take between De Klerk and his close associates, including G. F. la Croix, Piet Kramer, Margaret Kropholler, Johan van der Mey, J. F. Staal, and Hendrik Wijdeveld. All of these architects drew on a variety of sources to evolve their styles. They also developed a distinct ideology, and debate flourished between the Amsterdam School and other artistic tendencies on theoretical as well as stylistic differences. Actually, the success of the

Amsterdam School, particularly in Amsterdam, had much to do with the government's sympathy with its ideas, coupled with favorable economic circumstances.

The five articles published here deal with these various issues, each proceeding from a particular point of view. In "Amsterdam School: Definition and Delineation," the group's roots in the *Nieuwe Kunst* (the Dutch version of Art Nouveau) are discussed. This sets the stage for an exploration of the extent to which the expressionist Amsterdam School was in fact similar to those who have often been called its opponents, such as H. P. Berlage, who extended the influence of rationalism in Holland, promoting it as an alternative to the use of historical styles, or the abstract painters and architects of De Stijl. The supposed dissimilarities between these groups and persons, which have been posited on the basis of stylistic considerations and their written statements, are shown in this article to have proceeded from different interpretations of the same material. At the same time, by pointing out how, through the *Nieuwe Kunst*, the Amsterdam School was related to the Arts and Crafts movement in England, the opening essay of this study explains the interest of the school in such seemingly diverse architects as Frank Lloyd Wright, Erich Mendelsohn, Josef Hoffmann, and Bruno Taut.

How all these influences were assimilated is shown by Helen Searing in "The Formative Years of Michel de Klerk: Inspiration and Invention," in which she analyzes De Klerk's early work, including his competition designs made while he was still working as a draftsman for Eduard Cuypers and his first independent buildings. In the cultural milieu of Amsterdam, as well as through his apprenticeship in Cuypers's office, the young De Klerk became familiar with the work of Berlage, Mackintosh, the Arts and Crafts movement, and the Viennese Secession. Searing treats at great length De Klerk's competition entry for a cemetery of 1910, which, she says, "marked him as a young architect to be watched." In this project, De Klerk succeeded for the first time in developing his own style by combining all he had seen and learned in previous years.

In "Michel de Klerk: Utopia Built," Maristella Casciato takes a more theoretical approach, drawing upon the studies of the Italian scholar Manfredo Tafuri to argue that the idea of utopia serves to explain the way De Klerk imbued his architecture, especially his public housing, with meanings and symbols in order to arrest "the decline of the city's identity," which had begun in the nineteenth century. By elevating workers' housing to "workers' palaces," De Klerk and his Amsterdam School colleagues sought to restore the original character of the city, and, in the process, to confer dignity on the long-neglected workers.

The designs for interiors and decorative arts by members of the Amsterdam School are dealt with in the article by Petra Timmer. Because the Amsterdam School architects and designers saw the building as a total work of art, they extended to the interior design the same concerns and ideas that guided the architecture, including the ban on mechanical production. At the same time, they sought to link exterior and interior through the use of similar forms. Thus, the elaborate sculptural shapes found in their chimneys, balconies, towers, and so on, are echoed in their chairs, tables, mantelpieces, and such objects as clocks and mirrors. They further unified the interiors by repeating—in the furniture, textiles, objects—identical motifs in different ways. In view of the expensive handwork that such designs demanded, it should come as no surprise that the Amsterdam School architects were given no opportunities to realize such well-crafted interiors in their workers' housing.

The last article of the book, written by Karin Gaillard, deals with the political circumstances that enabled the Amsterdam School to produce such a large number of housing projects. At the beginning of the twentieth century, the government finally realized its responsibility to provide decent housing for workers at prices they could afford, but it did not take any action toward that goal until 1915. The maturing of its planning and favorable economic circumstances coincided with the rise of the Amsterdam School. The young Amsterdam School architects thus found themselves in a position to specialize in this type of construction. Indeed, several reports in architects' journals and archives testify that the head of

Amsterdam's Housing Authority, A. Keppler, asked the Amsterdam School architects, as a group, to design the new housing projects underwritten and overseen by his department. Keppler was attracted to these architects because, with their special attention to a decorative exterior, they endowed the workers' quarters with a unique character, giving the inhabitants a sense of pride and self-respect.

The Amsterdam School's involvement in creating these new areas was not restricted to building the houses. The municipal government commissioned the group to design a total urban environment—including bridges, benches, street lamps, mailboxes, and bookstalls, all embellished in accordance with its highly developed aesthetic principles. Thus, through their contacts with Keppler and other municipal authorities, the Amsterdam School architects were able to play a major role in shaping the special character of modern Amsterdam, where they remained active until the 1930s.

The exhibition and the plates in this book testify to the abundance and variety of the visual materials—drawings, photographs, graphic designs, models, and furniture—that have been preserved as the legacy of the Amsterdam School in Dutch archives, particularly in the Nederlands Documentatiecentrum voor de Bouwkunst in Amsterdam. De Klerk's work, reflecting his position in the school, forms the major portion of the exhibition, which consists of three sections. The first displays the designs of De Klerk's early years, as well as works by famous Dutch architects of the period, such as Berlage, De Bazel, and Kromhout, who were sources of inspiration; the second demonstrates De Klerk's growing prominence among the Dutch expressionist architects and the emergence of the Amsterdam School, shown by the work of Van der Mey, Kramer, Staal, and Wijdeveld, among others. The last gives De Klerk's late work until his death in 1923 and the flourishing of the Amsterdam School, as seen in housing complexes in different Amsterdam neighborhoods and in structures outside Amsterdam.

The expressive forms of the Amsterdam School suggest comparison with the current tendencies in architecture that once again employ decorative forms and reject the functionalist severity of the past decades. There are, however, differences between the two. The Amsterdam School belonged to the modernist trend because of its refusal to make use of traditional forms prevalent at the time, which today reappear in the work of the Post-Modernists. Moreover, the Dutch architects' refusal to accept the implications of industrial society is a stance that no contemporary architect of whatever persuasion can accept. It nonetheless seems appropriate to show the Amsterdam School's work at precisely this moment, when parochial attitudes toward form have broken down and we are once again able to appreciate the innovation and variety of this heretofore little-known group.

Overleaf: *Michel de Klerk. First block on the Spaarndammerplantsoen, Amsterdam, 1913–14. Rendering. Collection NDB, Amsterdam*

Michel de Klerk. Competition design for a mortuary chapel, 1910. Perspective. Collection NDB, Amsterdam

ONTWERP VOOR EEN
BLOK VOLKSWONINGEN
NIET UITGEVOERD.

ONTWERP VOOR EEN CLUBGEBOUW OP EEN SPORTTERREIN PERSPECTIVISCH AANZICHT.

MOTTO "DE 4DE"

Opposite: *Michel de Klerk. Competition design for a clubhouse, 1907. Perspective.* Collection NDB, Amsterdam

Michel de Klerk. Third block near the Spaarndammerplantsoen on Zaanstraat, Oostzaanstraat, and Hembrugstraat, Amsterdam, for Eigen Haard, 1917–21. Perspective view of the inner court, watercolor. Collection NDB, Amsterdam

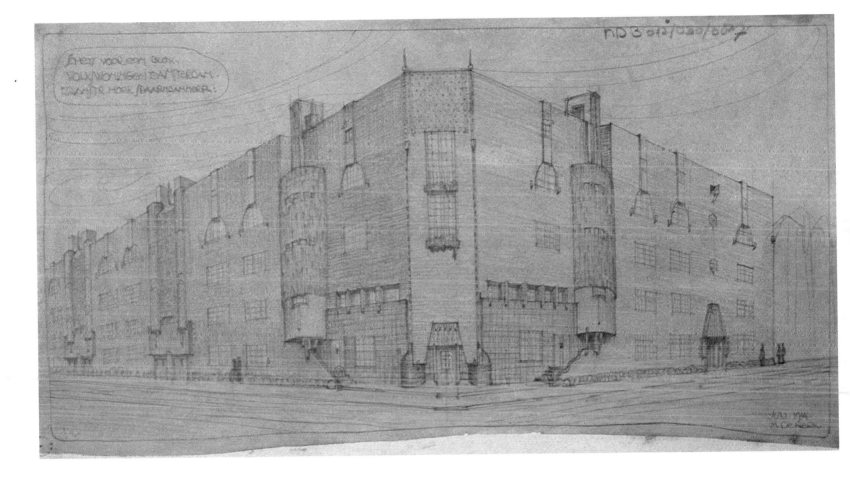

Opposite: *G. F. la Croix. Housing block on Bellamystraat and
Van Effenstraat, Amsterdam, 1917. Perspective, pencil, crayon,
and watercolor. Collection NDB, Amsterdam*

*Michel de Klerk. Second block on the Spaarndammerplantsoen,
Amsterdam, for Eigen Haard, 1914–16. Perspective, pencil and
crayon. Collection NDB, Amsterdam*

Michel de Klerk. Third block near the Spaarndammerplantsoen on Zaanstraat, Oostzaanstraat, and Hembrugstraat, Amsterdam, for Eigen Haard, 1917–21. Perspective view of Hembrugstraat, watercolor. Collection NDB, Amsterdam

Opposite: *D. Greiner. Public library in Betondorp, Amsterdam, 1924. Perspective, crayon. Collection NDB, Amsterdam*

Michel de Klerk. Design for a villa in Wassenaar, 1923. Perspective, pencil and wash. Collection NDB, Amsterdam

Michel de Klerk. Competition design for a high-rise building, c. 1920. Crayon and watercolor. Collection NDB, Amsterdam

Michel de Klerk. Competition design for a water tower in reinforced concrete, 1912. Watercolor and ink. Collection NDB, Amsterdam

Wim de Wit

THE AMSTERDAM SCHOOL: DEFINITION AND DELINEATION

THE history of twentieth-century Dutch architecture is generally conceived as a sequence of very distinct and often opposing groups. While a few architectural historians have suggested that the differences between these groups were not as great as one might have thought,[1] nobody has seriously examined the tendencies they represent in relation to one another. It is important to do so because such an undertaking enables us to recognize those characteristics that made each tendency quite unique and, with particular regard to the Amsterdam School, allows us to clarify the origins and significance of expressionism in Dutch architecture.

The Amsterdam School, an informally organized group of architects and designers centered around a magazine called *Wendingen*, was active between about 1915 and 1930, first in Amsterdam and later outside the Dutch capital as well.[2] During this period another group also came to the fore in Holland. This was De Stijl, a loose association of architects and painters who used the *De Stijl* magazine to propagate an abstract art with which an entirely new environment could be created.[3]

These groups have usually been described as radically different, if not indeed completely contradictory. With respect to the forms they produced this was indeed true. The buildings of the Amsterdam School are generally made of hand-formed brick and reveal a great plasticity in their forms; sculptural ornament and coloristic differentiation of the various materials (brick, tile,

C. J. Blaauw. Villa Meerhoek, Park Meerwijk, Bergen, 1917–18. From Wendingen 1, no. 8 (1918).
Opposite: *Plans of first and second floors*

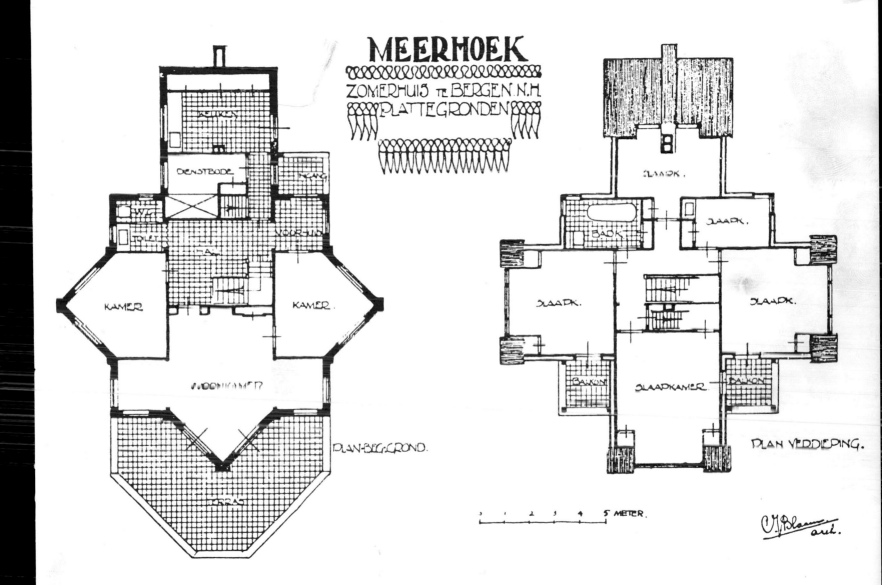

wood) play an essential role in the designs. The buildings designed by the architects of De Stijl, however, are often plain rectangular blocks of brick or concrete, which, apart from the occasional inclusion of color, are devoid of decoration; the play of volumes is intended to effectuate the plasticity of the whole.

Not only the buildings but also the writings of the Amsterdam School and De Stijl suggest that a large distance separated the two groups. Each denounced the other: De Stijl was declared "arrogant" because it claimed that its style was the only one possible, while the Amsterdam School was in turn condemned as "decadent" for its display of individual emotion. The crucial point of disagreement between the groups focused on whether a building should

embody and somehow signify the individual expression of the architect, as the Amsterdam School argued, or instead, according to De Stijl, whether all personal expression should be suppressed in a design that thus achieved universal validity.

These issues are clarified by a comparison made in the pages of *De Stijl* between two villas, one by an Amsterdam School architect and the other by a member of De Stijl.[4] The first was a house made of brick and wood with a thatched roof and a complex, multi-angled ground plan designed by C. J. Blaauw; this was contrasted with a Wrightian, flat-roofed, white cubical block of concrete construction by Rob van 't Hoff. Whereas Van 't Hoff's house was described as a manifestation

of a "fresh, tranquil, new spirit,"[5] Blaauw's was criticized for being more painterly and sculptural than it was architectural. Such polemical writing undoubtedly contributed a great deal toward establishing the image we have received of two groups opposed in the basic character of their work. However, the same article in *De Stijl* betrays a philosophical attitude that is also to be found throughout *Wendingen*: "A modern work of art, consciously made, is based on contemporary spiritual trends, so that the spirit of the time is reflected in it."[6] Even as he rejected De Stijl's claim to universality, Blaauw wrote in a manner that echoed the language and seemed to share the fundamental ideas expressed in the *De Stijl* passage quoted above: "It is precisely the nature of a 'style' that everybody sympathizes with it, understands it directly, because both artist and spectator develop in the same spirit and draw breath from the same atmosphere of sentiments."[7]

For both the Amsterdam School and the artists of De Stijl, a work of art had to express the essential character of contemporary society as a whole, and so testify to the existence of "communal art" *(Gemeenschapskunst)*. Furthermore, both groups considered the architect to be an artist capable of transcending the level of mere construction, the province of the engineer. Although the means envisioned by the Amsterdam School and De Stijl were different, the goal they aimed for was the same: the betterment of society through con-

Rob van 't Hoff. Villa Henny, Huis ter Heide, 1915–19. Collection NDB, Amsterdam

tact with art, which was considered good in its own right and also able to bestow goodness on anyone who encountered it. This meant that not only a painting or building, but the whole environment—the home, the street, the city—should be made into art. For the De Stijl group, the total design of the environment could be achieved only by means of a complete collaboration between artists and architects. The Amsterdam School architects, however, did not view collaboration as particularly valuable, and they considered themselves too individualistic to submit wholeheartedly to this principle. Although Amsterdam School architects often cooperated with sculptors and craftsmen, they regarded architecture as superior and therefore in a position to dictate to all the other arts.

In order to understand how these two groups, which on the surface appear to be so different, could in fact have so much in common, it is helpful to trace the origins of De Stijl and the Amsterdam School to their sources in the preceding generation. This will reveal not only how interrelated the Amsterdam School and De Stijl actually were, but also how the Amsterdam School related to such architects as H. P. Berlage and Bruno Taut. Finally, we will be in a position to analyze the Amsterdam School's notion of individual expression and to understand how it was achieved.

The roots of both the Amsterdam School and De Stijl can be found in the art movement of the period around the turn of the century. The then prevailing

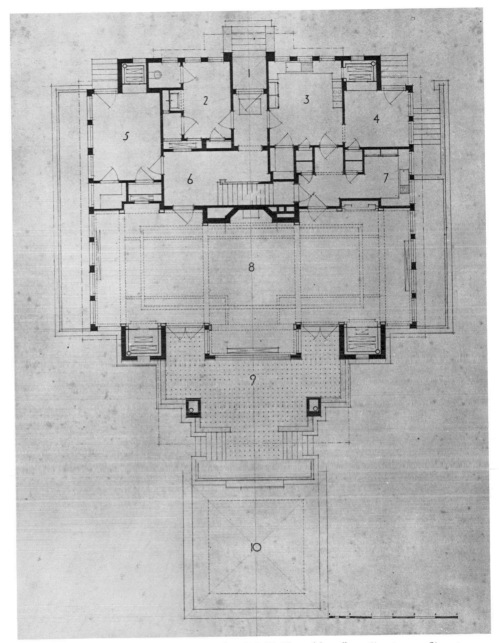

Rob van 't Hoff. Villa Henny, Huis ter Heide, 1915–19. Plan of first floor: 1) entrance; 2) coats; 3) kitchen; 4) sitting room; 5) study; 6) hall; 7) pantry; 8) living and dining room, 9) terrace, 10) pond. Print, Collection NDB, Amsterdam

Michel de Klerk. Portrait of the architects H. P. Berlage and K. P. C. de Bazel and of the painter Jan Toorop, n.d. Pencil. Collection NDB, Amsterdam

Opposite: *H. P. Berlage. Design for an electric chandelier based on a natural form, 1905. Watercolor. Collection NDB, Amsterdam*

Nieuwe Kunst, as the Dutch version of Art Nouveau was called, contained the seeds of many principles from which both movements would eventually develop. In a study devoted to book design that includes a general introduction to the *Nieuwe Kunst*, Ernst Braches describes how, during the period between 1892 and 1904, this movement attempted to avoid imitation of traditional styles in architecture and art, favoring instead the expression of ideas.[8] Just as art in the Middle Ages had been a reflection of an idea shared by every level of society, so, it was argued, the *Nieuwe Kunst* should in a symbolic way reflect the most essential thoughts current in society at the time. It was at this point that the notion of communal art emerged in Holland. In order to achieve this ideal, the architect had two means at his disposal. First of all, he could somehow endow the building materials with his spirit. In itself, material is a dead thing, but once invested with the spirit of the true artist, it comes to life. The individuality of the artist-architect[9] thus became an important element in the creative process. He considered himself to be a prophet; his was a rare talent capable of transforming useful materials into something beautiful, thereby making the world a better place in which to live.

The other means of achieving a communal art was to construct according to the principles of organic growth common to all forms in nature. Both designers and architects chose to model their works on the growth patterns of plants and crystals. Because the laws governing their growth were considered to be eternal, the *Nieuwe Kunst* designers and architects believed that in following these laws they would avoid ephemeral styles and tastes. To generate buildings and objects faithful to these eternal laws, many architects adopted Viollet-le-Duc's system of design based on a grid. The geometric character of the grid assured unity in the design just as the laws of nature guaranteed order in the organic world.

The *Nieuwe Kunst* thus consisted of two elements: on the one hand, there was a tendency to stress the artist's originality and spirituality, while, on the other, rationalist methods contributed to the universal validity of forms. The Amsterdam School and De Stijl each developed one of these components of the *Nieuwe Kunst*, and whatever differences existed between the two groups can in large part be ascribed to that fact. Whereas the De Stijl artist emphasized the universal values revealed by art, the Amsterdam School stressed the notion of the artist as a prophet, an individual endowed with the gift of special insight and therefore someone capable of recognizing essential truths and transmitting them to society as a whole. From this idea, the Amsterdam School developed a theory of individualistic expressionism, implicit in which was the notion that only after a deeply felt inward struggle would the work of art be born. The De Stijl artists' efforts to develop a universally valid expression, on the

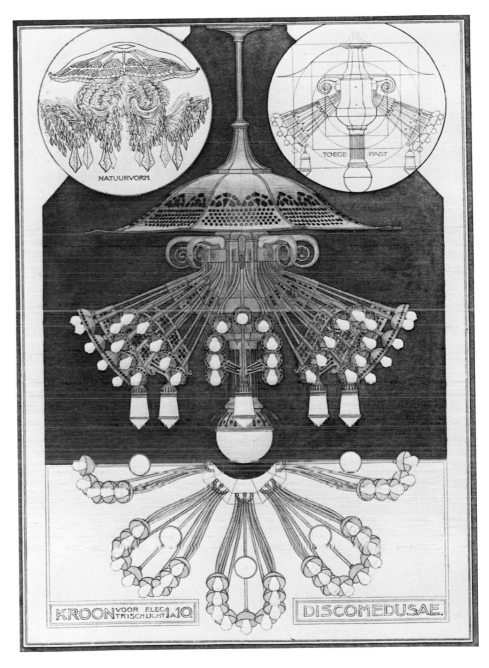

J. J. P. Oud. Housing block VIII in the Spangen district of Rotterdam, 1919–21. Photograph, Collection NDB, Amsterdam.   Opposite: *Standard ground plans and site plan*

other hand, resulted in a total abstraction, a denial of visible reality, which, they maintained, was merely a matter of individual perception. Therefore it was possible for the De Stijl group to accept the machine as a means of uniform production. The perfect finish of the machine-made object did not allow for expression of the artist's individuality. The very properties that De Stijl found so attractive in the machine were precisely the qualities for which the Amsterdam School found its use entirely unacceptable.

A comparison of two housing blocks, one by Michel de Klerk and the other by J. J. P. Oud, will further demonstrate what was involved in this difference between individuality and universality.[10] De Klerk's third block at the Spaarndammerplantsoen in Amsterdam (1917–21) is a particularly good example of architecture as an expression of the architect's idea, Oud's block VIII in the Spangen district of Rotterdam (1919–21), on the other hand, shows clearly what results when the architect tries to eliminate a sense of his own presence. The building by Oud consists of one long and two short sides of a city block. The long side has a flat roof, and for this and other reasons can be described as stylistically the most advanced. The short sides, with their pitched roofs and the symmetrical composition of each facade, look rather traditional. All sides show an accumulation of dwellings; no attempt was made to differentiate them. There is only one dwelling plan, which is end-

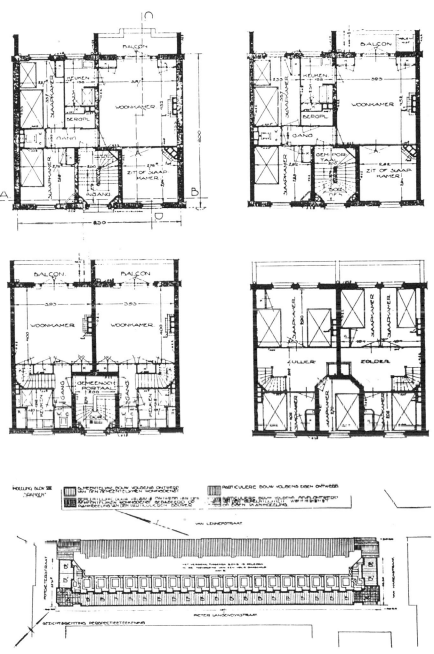

lessly—as if mechanically—repeated. In the facades, this repetition is expressed by the use of doors and windows with the same standard forms. The corners between the long and short sides of the square block are meant to function as interruptions in the repetitive character of the facades. Here, built-in balconies effect an alternation between open and closed surfaces, each of which in turn stands in a positive-negative relation to the long facade. The voids of the balconies, equal in height to the windows, have a negative aspect in relation to these windows, which act as positive elements in the facade. The parapets of the balconies relate in exactly the opposite way to the planes between the windows. This sort of play of volumes is probably what Oud was referring to when, in an article on standardization in architecture, he wrote that once standardization was in effect, "it will be possible to achieve beauty by creating contrasts of juxtaposed groups of volumes, doors, windows, etc., or of entire houses.... The architect acts as director, who stages the mass-produced objects in an architectural whole, an art of relations."[11]

De Klerk's third block at the Spaarndammerplantsoen contrasts directly with Oud's design. At no point in the three sides of his block did De Klerk suggest any form of mechanical production.[12] Indeed, he included more than fifteen different types of dwellings, an extreme of differentiation necessary to enable De Klerk to fit the interiors into the lively curves of his exteriors. Thus,

Michel de Klerk. Third block near the Spaarndammerplantsoen on Zaanstraat, Oostzaanstraat, and Hembrugstraat, Amsterdam, for Eigen Haard, 1917–21. Perspective view of Zaanstraat, watercolor. Collection NDB, Amsterdam. Hembrugstraat facade with tower, color pages 24–25

Michel de Klerk. Third block near the Spaarndammerplantsoen on Zaanstraat, Oostzaanstraat, and Hembrugstraat, Amsterdam, for Eigen Haard, 1917–21. Ground plan of the entire block, ink. Collection NDB, Amsterdam

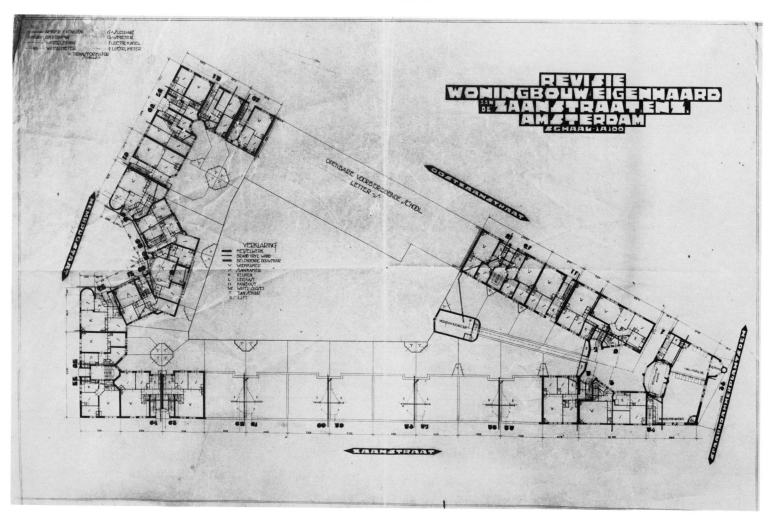

despite a large number of individual units, the block does not look at all like an accumulation of dwellings. On the contrary, it appears as if organically grown out of the soil. Its vitality is so forceful that at certain points, for example, above the doors or in the attic, it seems to burst forth in swollen forms on the facade. In an essay about De Klerk's work, K. P. C. de Bazel described this effect in a somewhat different but related way: "every form lives...like a strained membrane, a skin, in which a bone, a tendon presses outward, in which a nervous spasm, a vein, a ripple of an organ makes itself felt plastically. His work shows a search for an organically suggestive expression of life."[13] How literally this expression of life was conceived becomes clear as

soon as one looks at the ground plan. In the center of the inner courtyard is a little building intended for the meetings of the housing association Eigen Haard, which gave the commission to build the block: the grantor of life in this housing block is placed in its midst like a heart in a body.

The well-known tower on the Hembrugstraat side must be seen in the same terms. It has no function and there is no way to enter it. But because of its recessed position, it appears to grow out of the interior of the block and thus functions as a sign to the outside world of the life that goes on within. At the same time it is also a proud emblem of a particularly social character, conveying a sense of the position that the working inhabitants have attained

Michel de Klerk. Three blocks on and near the Spaarndammerplantsoen, Amsterdam, 1913–21. Site plan, ink. Collection NDB, Amsterdam

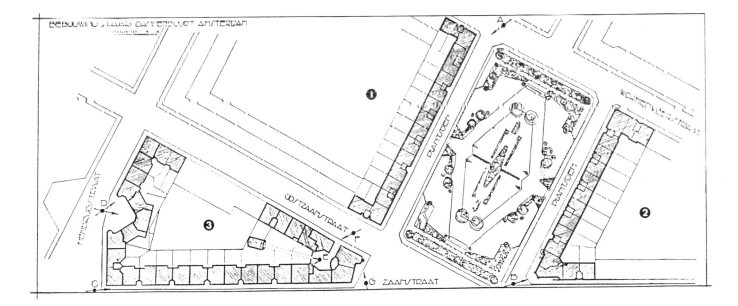

Michel de Klerk. Second block on the Spaarndammerplantsoen, Amsterdam, for Eigen Haard, December 1914. Perspective. From Bouwkundig Weekblad, *1915*

through their housing.[14] The tower, thus conceived, can be said to mediate between the pure creativity of the architect's subjective expression and the social group whose dwellings he designs. Individualized form here gives shape to collective identity in a manner that cannot be realized in Oud's accumulation of mechanically repeated units.

Although the Amsterdam School and De Stijl had in common their respective origins in the *Nieuwe Kunst*, and, it has been argued, the fundamental principles of both groups betray the influence of H. P. Berlage—the most important Dutch architect at the turn of the century, when the *Nieuwe Kunst* style was at its height—recent scholarship has shown that Eduard Cuypers was in fact more significant for the development of the Amsterdam School.[15] This helps to explain the origin of the Amsterdam School's individualistic interpretation of communal art, which De Klerk, Piet L. Kramer, and a number of others began to develop while working as draftsmen in Cuypers's office. Berlage's notion of communal art was, in comparison, more concerned with society as a whole and, in particular, with the expression of his socialist convictions. Moreover, Berlage's rational approach to design, stressing the role of function and construction in determining the form of a building, generally precluded individualistic manifestations.[16] Indeed, his rationalism prompted Berlage to emphasize a *zakelijke* ("objective") atti-

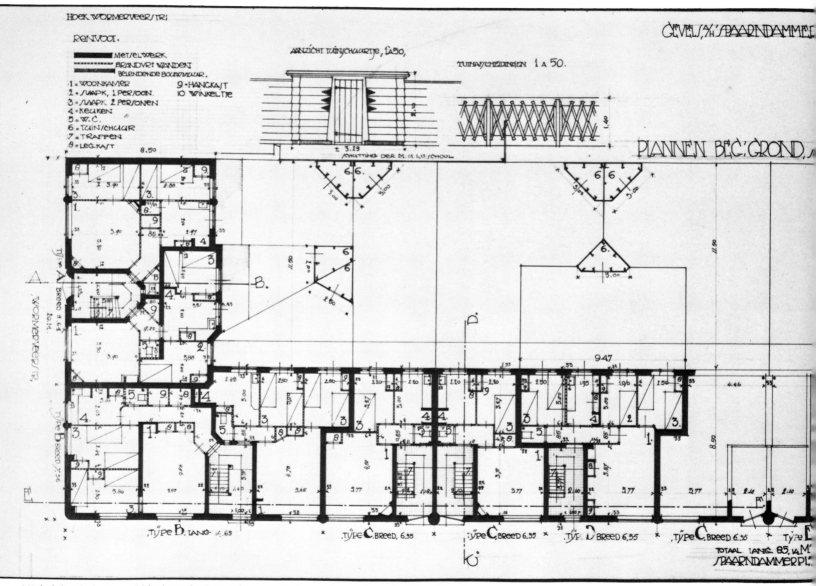

Michel de Klerk. Second block on the Spaarndammerplantsoen, Amsterdam, for Eigen Haard,
1914–16. Plan of the first floor, ink. Collection NDB, Amsterdam

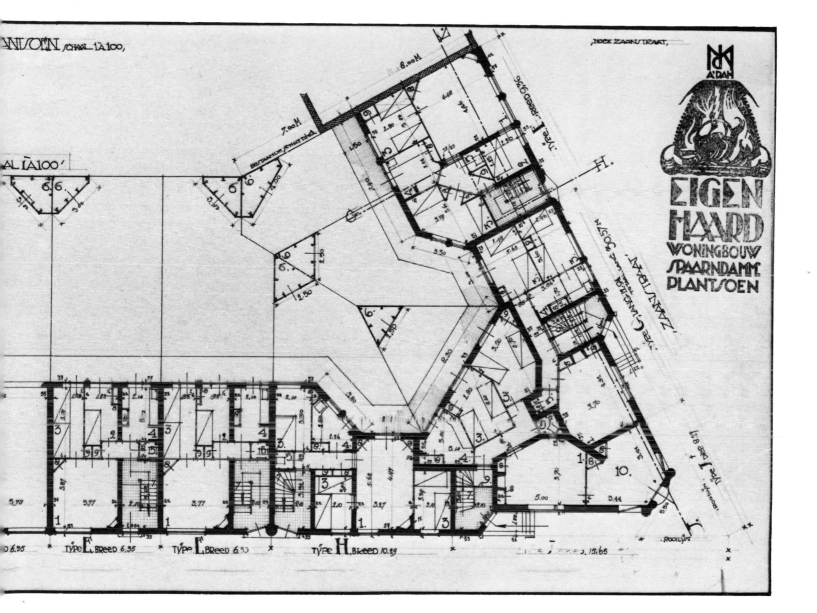

J. L. M. Lauweriks. Installation of an exhibition of Christian art, Dusseldorf, 1913. Gouache. Collection NDB, Amsterdam

tude toward building practice.

The principle of subjective expression hinted at by Cuypers was, however, consciously developed by other architects of Cuypers's and Berlage's generation, namely K. P. C. de Bazel, J. L. M. Lauweriks, and W. Kromhout.

At the turn of the century Kromhout was a staunch adherent of a rationalism, based on the theories of Viollet-le-Duc, that, he argued, reflected the spirit of the time. But later, the personal mark of the architect in the form a building takes and the materials with which it is made became increasingly important for Kromhout. By 1913 he was describing the practice of design as an inherently individualistic process in much the same words as the Amsterdam School architects would use five years later. For Kromhout, a design could only be generated by a vision of forms "which one, in a struggle, tries to distill into something tangible, by means of that wonderfully difficult act—formal composition, in which, avoiding banality, one tries to remain in a state of mind as lofty as the forms one envisions."[17] The Amsterdam School architects must have known Kromhout's ideas; he lectured frequently at the society Architectura et Amicitia, of which they all were members.

Even more important than Kromhout had been for the formation of the Amsterdam School were the *Nieuwe Kunst* architects De Bazel and Lauweriks, both of whom permitted decoration in their rationalist designs, as long as it fitted within the geometric grid with which they always worked. The influence of Lauweriks in particular went far beyond the realm of theory. He was actively involved with the foundation of *Wendingen*, the magazine that functioned as the mouthpiece of the Amsterdam School between 1918 and 1925.[18] It may seem paradoxical to speak of the active involvement of someone who lived outside Holland from 1904 until 1916, precisely the period when the ideas of the Amsterdam School were taking shape. However, during these years, which he spent in Germany, Lauweriks maintained contact with his colleagues in Holland and occasionally published articles in Dutch magazines; in turn, Dutch architects followed Lauweriks's activities abroad with great interest.

Lauweriks's stay in Germany is most often cited for the influence that his grid method then had on an internationally important range of architects, including Peter Behrens, Walter Gropius, and Le Corbusier,[19] but in the context of this discussion what needs to be emphasized is Lauweriks's proximity to the development of expressionist trends evident in German architecture of the prewar years. Dutch architects were made aware of Lauweriks's involvement in the German movement during the course of a lecture that he delivered in Amsterdam in 1915, a year before he returned to work there as director of the Quellinus School, an arts and crafts school.[20] Upon his return, Lauweriks was invited to join the editorial staff of the magazine *Architectura*. His ap-pointment coincided with the reorganization of this journal into the monthly review *Wendingen*, and although H. Th. Wijdeveld, who would become *Wendingen*'s editor-in-chief, was in large part responsible for the mechanics of this transformation, Lauweriks was without doubt its source of inspiration.[21]

As a member of *Wendingen*'s editorial staff, during the next several years Lauweriks was in a position to define and promote a discussion that was central to the concerns of the Amsterdam School. In "Communal Art and Individualism,"[22] Lauweriks, as the title of this article suggests, attempted to combine the *Nieuwe Kunst* idea of communal art with the notion of individualism, which, as we have seen, the Amsterdam School considered to be the only means of revitalizing architecture. He remarked that, although at that time different styles were available, eventually these would be subsumed in an aesthetic unity transcending any particular style. Thus, he believed, it would be a communal art, for, indeed, any true art must be communal "in the sense that it draws on a spiritual reservoir of a higher order and, after having condensed the ideas thus gained into a vision assimilated as an artistic impression, finally embodies them in the work of art."[23] Such a state, however, could only be achieved in a society that, like the medieval one, was characterized by shared social and cultural concerns, toward the realization of which every member of society was

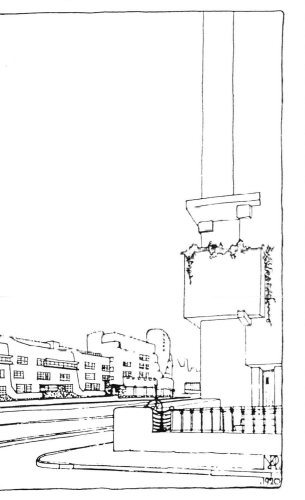

Michel de Klerk and Piet Kramer. Housing block on Pieter Lodewijk Takstraat, Amsterdam, for De Dageraad, 1919–21. Perspective, ink. Collection NDB, Amsterdam

willing to collaborate.

At this point, Lauweriks's argument took an unexpected turn: he stated that, although everyone would be absorbed by a single communal ideal, each person would also retain his individual integrity. Lauweriks sought to resolve the apparent contradiction between his idea of communal art and that of individualism by distinguishing three sorts of individualism: "lower individualism," which he identified with primitive societies; "pure individualism," characteristic of his own milieu, and which he identified with selfishness; and, finally, a transcendent "super individualism," elevated above any egocentric ambition. The attainment of super individualism would necessarily be accompanied by the blossoming of communal art.[24]

That the issues raised by Lauweriks were seen as a challenge, a spur to the development of the work and ideas of many Amsterdam School architects, is made readily evident by other articles in *Wendingen*. In a series of three articles entitled "Architecture and Society,"[25] J. M. van der Mey articulated a belief he shared with Lauweriks that good architecture could only come about if equilibrium between the individual and society were maintained; given this circumstance, the architect would be able to exercise his individual genius in the interest of bettering society—but with the crucial precondition that society must in turn already have reached a level in which the architect's individual genius could blossom and

mature. In view of Van der Mey's awareness of what he condemned as the "unfeeling indifference" of the national government, it is not likely that he believed that a good, communal architecture would ever be achieved.

It was J. B. van Loghem who actually brought this discussion onto a political level. Van Loghem cannot be considered a member of the Amsterdam School, but he was on the editorial board of *Wendingen* during the first years of the magazine's existence. In the article he published there in response to Lauweriks, he attempted to move the discussion on communal art from the philosophical realm to that of practical reality.[26] Rather than a vision of communal art arising as it were spontaneously at some undefined future moment as the embodiment of a unified social structure, Van Loghem saw communal art as the product of the actual work performed by architects for the benefit of the community. He noted that the first step in this direction could be seen in the new involvement with housing on the part of virtually all architects toward the end of the First World War. Unlike so many others, Van Loghem did not protest state regulations governing the building of housing blocks; on the contrary, he believed that the government's strong hand was necessary to the attainment of communal art. By imposing strict building regulations, paradoxically the state secured the possibility of individual freedom and created a situation in which the artist, Van Loghem argued, was "supported by the community."

Thus far no one had succeeded in explaining precisely how communal art and individuality could be reconciled. Aware that this was the case, Blaauw declared that he did not even know what communal art meant: art *for* or art *by* the community? Unable to share Van Loghem's belief in the positive effects of government intervention in architectural practice, Blaauw was in effect attacking the validity of communal art, which he thought would curtail the architect's freedom, for example, by establishing rules for standardization. "It is impossible," Blaauw wrote, "for an artist to strive consciously toward communal art without losing his artistry, his personality."[27]

The whole discussion was finally closed by two articles, one by De Bazel and the other by Lauweriks. In his analysis of De Klerk's architecture, De Bazel showed how closely related his ideas were to those of the Amsterdam School.[28] He began with a very clear explanation of communal art and individualism, maintaining that inherent in the design process itself was an individualistic element. Because the architect was always bound to a commission, De Bazel believed, he always had to struggle "in order to see his own deeper essence, which is a reflection of the universal existence, reconstituted in his work, while still respecting the building's own purpose."[29] Only the true artist, possessing a pure intuition, attained an enlightened attitude cor-

responding to the building's purpose; only he would be able to give shape to the "rhythm of the time." De Bazel accepted individualism as characteristic of an architect's work, but for him it always had to be at the service of a larger purpose: the expression of universal values of the era in which the architect lived.

Two months after De Bazel's article appeared, Lauweriks published an essay entitled "The Titanic Aspects of Art," in which the notion of communal art is scarcely mentioned, and individualism prevails. Here Lauweriks described the creative work of an architect as a difficult struggle, comparing it to the battle of the Titans against the gods. The creative act was so difficult, he wrote, because it involved "a transposition from a spiritual to a sensory realm, or the fixing in a visible form of something that does not exist."[30]

From this point on, expressionistic individualism was openly acknowledged to be the main characteristic of the thinking of the Amsterdam School, and until 1925 it was proclaimed in every volume of *Wendingen*. But communal art continued to be an essential component of the credo of these architects, and on a deeper level it remained an important element of their work. Everyone who wrote in *Wendingen* subscribed to the communal ideal, conceding that individualism could not be a goal in itself but was only a surrogate until the ideal society became real.

Anticipation of an ideal society of the future took two forms. First was an

expectation that the period after the First World War, which had caused so much suffering, would inevitably be a happier time; this idea was reinforced by knowledge of the revolutions in Russia and Germany. Paradoxically, anticipation also took the shape of a nostalgic, retrospective vision of the Middle Ages as a model for the future.

Advanced artists in Holland were very much interested in the political upheavals that occurred elsewhere in Europe at the end of the First World War. Although without mentioning them directly, Wijdeveld went so far as to insert a passage about the revolutions in a December 1918 article that ostensibly had nothing to do with the subject: "Now that the entire world's social structure—which had been unable to prevent endless suffering—is rocking to its foundations....now that the revolutionary fire has begun to tremble in the human soul, as a liberating passion, as a blessing spirit—who could have presumed that in our times of violence and deep anguish....suddenly a shout of joy would rise up out of the hearts of the multitude. We stand on the threshold of great times, in which the ideals we once considered utopian will be realized."[31] Another remark implying expectation of some sort of revolution can be found in Wijdeveld's introduction to an issue of *Wendingen* devoted to workers' housing. Here Wijdeveld openly stated that really new architecture could come about only in a new society. "The recovery [of housing]" he wrote, "will only come about after a thorough remodeling of the social structure. Only a new society—that is, a return to an ordered relationship between human beings, a new family life, a developing new world order—will make a beginning in the direction of real housing for the people."[32] In light of this passage, one might well ask if the architects of the Amsterdam School were communists or revolutionary socialists. The answer is that they were neither. The expectation of realignment in the social hierarchy after the First World War corresponded well with the idea of a communal art. Revolution would finally bring about the new society in which every individual would be inspired by the same ideals, thus providing a context in which a new architecture would come into existence. It is because they believed in this kind of idealized revolution, and not because of any deeply held political convictions, that these architects were interested in the events taking place in Russia after 1917. A revolution of the spirit was much more important for the Amsterdam School than a revolution of society's structure from capitalism to communism.[33]

Through R. N. Roland Holst, who was on the editorial board of *Wendingen* and whose wife was an active member of the Dutch Communist Party, the architects of the Amsterdam School did have direct contact with communist ideas. It was probably through Roland Holst that the program of art education run by the Soviet Directorate for the Elevation of the People came to be published in *Wendingen*.[34] The introduction to this program, probably written by Roland Holst, suggests the close relationship between the value that communism attached to art and the ideal of a communal art advocated by the Amsterdam School: "The Directorate has provided a summary of a program clearly showing that the intention of the Russian Communists is to bring art once and for all back to the community from which it originated.... She [the Soviet Republic] brings the artist to life, so that life will be beautiful and art will be living."[35] It was because he shared these same expectations of a new and better life that the socialist director of Amsterdam's municipal housing board engaged Michel de Klerk, Piet Kramer, H. Th. Wijdeveld, J. F. Staal, and others, who were already being referred to as the Amsterdam School, in the building of housing blocks. These commissions were given during the First World War and in the first years thereafter, when the architects of the Amsterdam School were still young; most had only recently begun or were then just starting their independent careers. The great building activity of the municipality in this period was therefore a welcome source of work, all the more so because other commissions were virtually unavailable at that time. However, the architects of the Amsterdam School were not as socially involved as often has been assumed. The socialist municipal government sought them out, not the other way around. If the economic situation in the Netherlands had been different, the architects of the Amsterdam School would not as a matter of course have decided to build only housing blocks. Although the emphasis on a communal art necessarily carried with it a social vision, that vision was very much abstracted from any particular social condition and often seems to have been more rhetoric than it was a substantive program for change.

The anticipation of a better world to be achieved once the war ended had its counterpart in a retrospective longing for the ideal social fabric of the Middle Ages. In this tendency to eulogize the past, the Amsterdam School exposed its roots in the thinking of Ruskin, Morris, and the Arts and Crafts movement, all of whom looked to the Medieval Gothic as a style signifying, just as it resulted from, the working together of artists and craftsmen.[36] In *Wendingen*, the history of architecture was often described as a continuous alternation of two tendencies: an idealistic, classical architecture, composed according to eternal laws, and an expressionistic gothic that allowed each craftsman with his own subjective will to make a contribution to a collective art, of which the cathedral became the symbol.[37] By exercising his intention, his ability to pervade the materials with his spirit, the craftsman insured that every aspect of the building would be elevated above inert substance, and, when taken together, all the various elements of the building would forge a whole that embodied the spirit of the age. In the

J. C. van Epen. Design for a crystalline high-rise building, c. 1920. Crayon and watercolor. Collection NDB, Amsterdam

Amsterdam School's vision of the Middle Ages, this notion of spiritualization was even more important than the ideal of communal art, for which they also revered the medieval period.

It should come as no surprise that the Amsterdam School gave a very individualistic and expressionistic interpretation to the notion of spiritualization, which they defined as a struggle to identify the spirit of the time, to embody this spirit in a palpable form, and, finally, to so work the form that it transcends its own material substance, thus becoming a pure expression of the original idea. The architects themselves recognized the difficulties inherent in this process. The very materials with which they worked, whether stone, brick, or wood, and the functions their buildings had to fulfill imposed barriers to spiritualization that were not found in other means of artistic expression. Painting, for example, was considered to be more spiritual than architecture, but the most spiritual of all the arts were dance and drama (including the marionette theater), because in them the spirit of the artist could be translated directly; indeed, they were thought of as pure expression.

In several articles in *Wendingen* devoted to these arts, Wijdeveld evoked a notion of spiritualization involving the rejection of all natural and figurative forms in favor of an abstract art. In his opinion, traditional theater was limited to imitation of daily life. Only by omitting all reference to nature and the human figure could the artist give direct expression to his feelings. Just how Wijdeveld understood this expressionistic theater becomes clear in a text about marionettes, which he considered to be dead "because they are material, but which all of a sudden can become entirely spirit when pervaded by our thought or will....Should the new drama be performed in rags and tatters, with wood and glue, with the help of cords and strings...yes...strings especially!...in order to reach the spiritual threads that are controlled from one point?"[38] A more explicit description of the artist as prophet is hardly imaginable: Wijdeveld credited him with direct contact with God.

For the architect, such an immediate form of expression was not possible. His art was not abstract; on the contrary, it was very much involved with materials which it was the architect's task to elevate above the demands of mere construction, molding them according to his own insight and intent. This notion of molding was conceived quite literally: many architects of the Amsterdam School started the design process by making a sketchy model in clay or plaster. In so doing they tried to fashion the building as a whole, together with all its details, into sculpture. They called this process "artification of the form" and "formal will." Neither resistance of materials nor the laws of gravity were taken into account. Instead, they believed that the whole building should become a piece of sculpture and give the impression that it was grown organically, like a shell or

Michel de Klerk. Competition design for a high-rise building, 1915. Perspective, pencil, colored pencil, and crayon. Collection NDB, Amsterdam. Color page 28

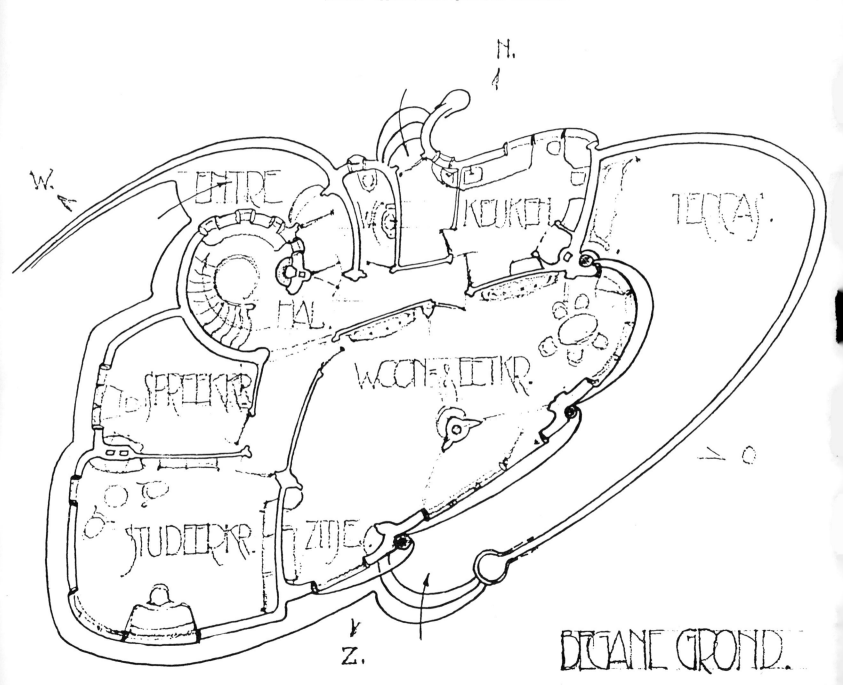

A. Eibink and J. A. Snellebrand. *Design for a country house in the dunes, 1917. Ink and crayon. Collection NDB, Amsterdam.* Below: *Plan of the first floor;* opposite, above: *south and north facades;* opposite, below: *plan of the second floor*

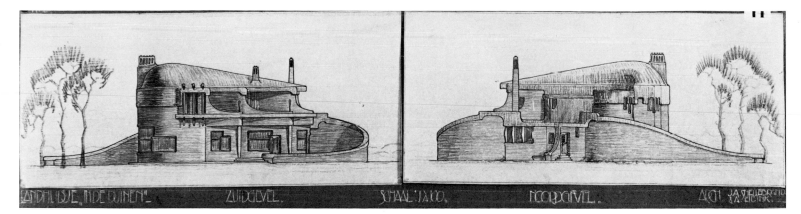

LANDHUISJE "IN DE DUINEN"   ZUIDGEVEL.   SCHAAL 1 À 100.   NOORDGEVEL.   ACHT J.A. SNELLEBRAND J.A. PLEITER

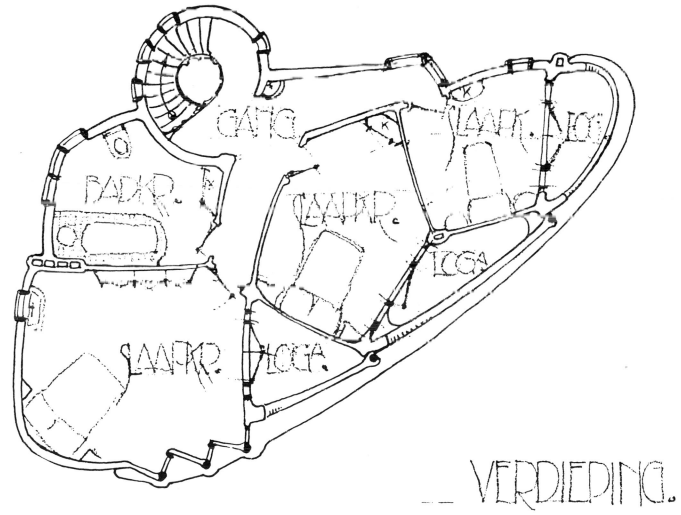

VERDIEPING.

A. Eibink and J. A. Snellebrand. Competition design for a church in Elshout, 1915. Perspective, pencil. Collection NDB, Amsterdam. Opposite: Ground plan, ink and crayon

a crystal.[39]

Indeed, the spontaneous growth of certain organic creatures was considered to be the best example for construction. The Amsterdam School architects admired the freedom and boldness of the forms that sea mollusks, for example, create when enveloping themselves in their shells, thus producing enclosing spaces that grow out of an inner impulse according to the mollusks' own needs. Occasionally, architects tried to imitate this, making shell-like ground plans, as in A. Eibink and J. A. Snellebrand's country house, where even the walls are drawn like vertebrae. Crystals aroused even more interest because their transparency and sparkle suggested the characteristics that glass architecture should ideally exhibit. "Like a polished crystal, with all its sides full of sparkle and color: that is how these younger architects see the building."[40] The crystal was also a metaphor for the ideas that crystallize in the architect's mind, to which he gives shape in his buildings. On a cover of *Wendingen* designed by Roland Holst, an architect mediates between an image of a building shaped like a crystal, which he holds in his hands, and the crystalline form of the surrounding universe.[41]

Although they extolled glass and used it within their buildings, for the Amsterdam School glass never became the predominant structural material that it was for Bruno Taut and other German expressionists of the period. Instead, the Amsterdam School favored

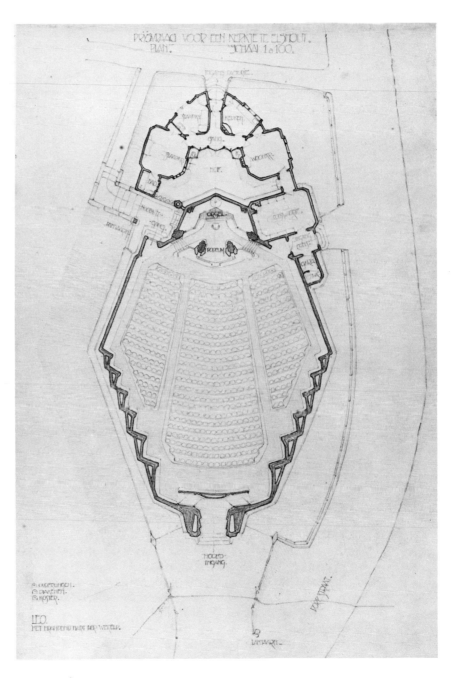

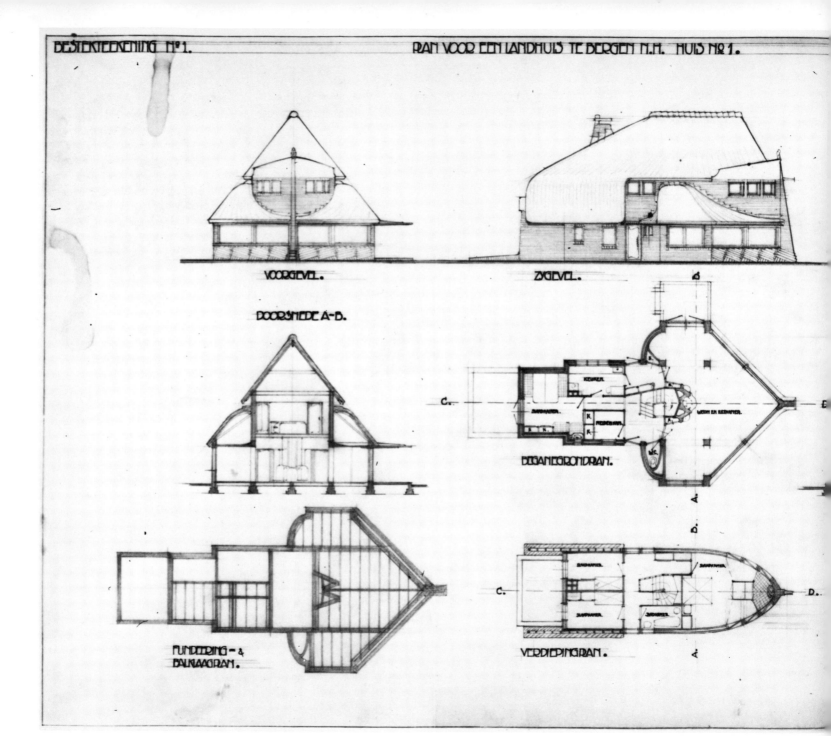

BESTEKTEEKENING N°1.　　　　　PLAN VOOR EEN LANDHUIS TE BERGEN N.H. HUIS N°1.

VOORGEVEL.　　　　　ZIJGEVEL.

DOORSNEDE A–B.

BEGANEGRONDPLAN.

FUNDEERING- & BALKLAAGPLAN.

VERDIEPINGPLAN.

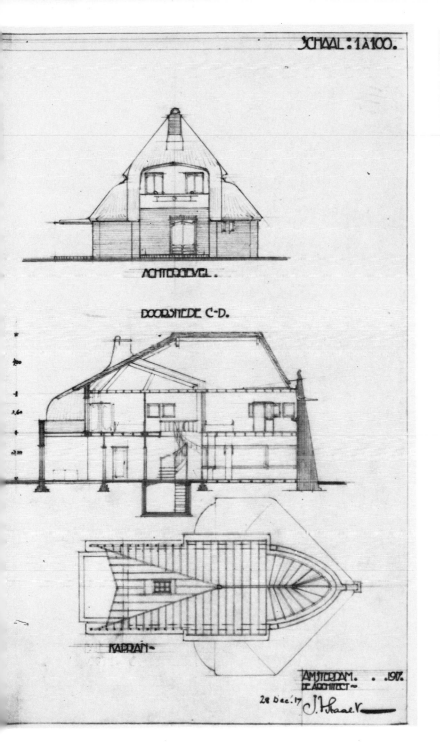

ACHTERGEVEL.

DOORSNEDE C-D.

KAPPLAN.

AMSTERDAM. . .1917.
DE ARCHITECT

28 Dec. '17

J. F. Staal. Country house De Bark, Park Meerwijk, Bergen, 1917–18.
Opposite: *Plans and facades, ink, crayon, and pencil.*
Collection NDB, Amsterdam

brick for its natural properties; moreover, the fact that brick could be made by hand allowed for it to assume some very exceptional, particularized forms. In order to realize an expressive, sculptural architecture, the Amsterdam School recognized that concrete would have been an even more appropriate material: "because reinforced concrete can absorb forces coming from all sides and redirect them…[it] can be transformed, so to speak, from a dead material into a living organism."[42] Unfortunately, however, building techniques were not yet so advanced that concrete could actually be used in this way.[43]

It is readily apparent that the Amsterdam School shared many social ideals with the German expressionist architects, who also emerged as a self-conscious group just prior to the First World War. Not only the Werkbund, founded in Munich in 1907, but also several organizations established during

H. Th. Wijdeveld. Design for a People's Theater in the Vondelpark, Amsterdam, 1919.
Perspective, print. Collection NDB, Amsterdam

P. Vorkink and Jac. Ph. Wormser. Country house 't Reigersnest, Oostvoorne, 1918.
Model, plaster. Collection NDB, Amsterdam

M. Kropholler. Housing block on Holendrechtstraat and Uithoornstraat, Amsterdam, 1921–22.
Perspective. Drawing by A. J. Westerman. From Amsterdamse Bouwkunst 1815–1940 *by H. J. F. de*
Roy van Zuydewijn (Amsterdam, 1970).   Opposite: *Detail of completed building*

the revolution that followed the war in 1918 functioned as important arenas for the development of expressionist attitudes in Germany. In particular, through the Arbeitsrat für Kunst (Work Council for Art) and the November-gruppe, such architects as Walter Gropius and Bruno Taut gave voice to concepts of architecture similar to the ideas of the Amsterdam School. Common to all was a conception of the practice of architecture as an aesthetic enterprise capable of establishing an ideal environment for society as a whole while at the same time expressing the formal intentions of an individual designer. Although it is important to recognize their similarities, one major difference between the Dutch and the German expressionists takes us much further toward specifying the particular significance of the Amsterdam School. For lack of both financial and material resources in the immediate postwar period, German architects, with few exceptions, were unable to build, while in Holland, which had maintained neutrality during the war, conditions were much more favorable. German Expressionism was largely confined to paper (words and drawings were its principal mediums); in Holland, however, social and economic circumstances created a climate that was particularly conducive to the vision of the Amsterdam School architects, who consequently built on an enormous scale during these years. Moreover, the utopian trend in German architecture was exceptionally brief, lasting only from 1918 until 1920.

Thereafter, because of a continuing absence of building commissions, utopianism gradually gave way to disillusionment. By the time the German economy began its recovery in 1923, architects had abandoned the expressionism that characterized their designs of the immediate postwar years in favor of a more sober, rational approach that would enable them to build as much and as frugally as possible.[44]

At just about the same time, around 1923, the national government in Holland changed its building policy, allotting less money to housing associations and municipalities so that, in the absence of public funding, the building of housing blocks would be assumed by a revived private sector. However, entrepreneurs were unwilling to underwrite the expense involved in creating individualized, expressive forms. Therefore, from this moment onward, Amsterdam School architects were forced to use standardized elements and new techniques that would reduce the costs of building. The wealth of materials necessary to realize the voluminous forms in the early years was no longer affordable. As a result, the facades of the blocks were more and more often designed as flat surfaces in which only such elements as bay windows and rhythmic compositions of apertures were used to convey a relatively limited sense of liveliness. Thus, the Amsterdam School architects were gradually forced to assume a more realistic attitude toward design. This gradual transformation was eventually reflected in *Wendingen*, where expressionist ideas ceased to find an outlet after 1925–26. The following year, a complete change of editorial staff brought an end to the original expressionistic character of the magazine, transforming it into a mere picture album devoid of any collective idea.

This study of the Amsterdam School in its social and historical context should enable us to understand better the special significance of the group. For too long its architecture has been seen merely as an accumulation of eccentric forms to which ground plans were forced to conform. It should by now be clear that what at first sight appear to be impossibly complicated forms are in fact meant to express an idea: the life in the building. For the Amsterdam School the expression of ideas was more important than a study of rationalized housing needs leading to the development of a new type of ground plan.

The significance that the Amsterdam School attached to expressive form is also to be seen in the special attention that these architects bestowed on the medium of drawing. The entire design process can be read in their drawings, from the first preliminary sketch, through the perspective, to the detailing of the brick decoration. It was Michel de Klerk in particular who, through the extraordinary quality of his watercolors, set the high standard that prompted other architects of the Amsterdam School to achievements of equal merit.

NOTES

I would like to express my gratitude to my wife, Nancy Troy, for her advice and support and, above all, for all the hours she spent helping me avoid the pitfalls of English grammar.

1. R. Banham, *Theory and Design in the First Machine Age* (New York: Praeger, 1960); Giovanni Fanelli, *Architettura Moderna in Olanda 1900–1940* (Florence: Marchi e Bertolli, 1968), rev. ed. *Moderne architectuur in Nederland 1900–1940* (The Hague: Staatsuitgeverij, 1978).

2. The earliest mention of this name dates from 1916; see *Nederlandse architectuur 1910–1930 Amsterdamse School* (Amsterdam: Stedelijk Museum, 1975), p 51. Other important studies of the Amsterdam School include Suzanne S. Frank, "Michel de Klerk (1884–1923): An Architect of the Amsterdam School" (Ph.D. diss., Columbia University, 1969), Helen E. Searing, "Housing in Holland and the Amsterdam School" (Ph.D. diss., Yale University, 1971).
   Wendingen was published in twelve volumes between 1918 and 1931. For the history of *Wendingen*, see note 18. See also Giovanni Fanelli and Ezio Godoli, eds., *Wendingen 1918–1931, Documenti dell'arte olandese del Novecento* (Florence: Centro Di, 1982).

3. *De Stijl* was published between 1917 and 1932. Recent publications devoted to De Stijl include M. Friedman, ed., *De Stijl: Visions of Utopia* (Minneapolis: Walker Art Center; New York: Abbeville Press, 1982); Carel Blotkamp, ed., *De Beginjaren van De Stijl* (Utrecht: Reflex, 1982); Giovanni Fanelli, *De Stijl* (Bari: Laterza, 1983); Nancy J. Troy, *The De Stijl Environment* (Cambridge, Mass.: The MIT Press, 1983).

4. V. Huszar, "Aesthetische Beschouwingen," *De Stijl* 2, no. 3 (1919), pp. 27–30.

5. Ibid, p 29.

6. Ibid., p. 27.

7. C. J. Blaauw, "Over moderne theorieën en bouwkunstbeoefening," *Wendingen* 3, no. 1 (1920), pp. 13–14. "The spirit of the time" was first used by the Austrian art historian Alois Riegl. It was taken up by Dutch artists and architects of different tendencies, but none of them defined what the phrase actually meant to them.

8. Ernst Braches, *Het Boek als Nieuwe Kunst, Een Studie in Art Nouveau* (Utrecht: Oosthoek, 1973). The following paragraphs are based on this book.

9. In Dutch, a distinction can be made between the words *architect* and *bouwkundige* ("builder"). The *architect* considers himself to be artistically involved, whereas the *bouwkundige* concerns himself only with building construction.

10. It should be borne in mind that De Klerk and Oud are discussed here both as individual architects and as exponents of their groups, although what is said about their work is not necessarily valid for all their colleagues throughout the period in which the Amsterdam School and De Stijl were active.

11. J. J. P. Oud, "Bouwkunst en Normalisatie bij den Massabouw," *De Stijl* 1, no. 7 (1918), p. 79.

12. See also Maristella Casciato and Wim de Wit, *Le case Eigen Haard di Michel de Klerk 1913–1921* (Rome: Officina, 1983)

13. K. P. C. de Bazel, "Onze tijd en het werk van M. de Klerk," *Wendingen* 2, no. 2 (1919), p. 7.

14. It is striking that in his watercolor drawing of the Hembrugstraat, De Klerk indicates a decorative element at the top of the tower in the shape of a rooster. For many years the rooster was the symbol of the Dutch Social Democrats. It was also the symbol of the socialist housing association De Dageraad (The Dawn) for which De Klerk, together with Piet L. Kramer, built another large housing complex. The crowing rooster announces at dawn the new day, that is, a new life after the revolution.

15. Helen Searing, "Berlage or Cuypers? The Father of Them All," in: Helen Searing, ed., *In Search of Modern Architecture: A Tribute to Henry-Russell Hitchcock* (New York: The Architectural History Foundation; Cambridge, Mass.: The MIT Press, 1982, pp. 226–43.).

16. In their turn, the Amsterdam School architects did not accept Berlage's rationalism. Wijdeveld, for example, described the Amsterdam School as "visionaries who play inoffensively with the treasures of rationalism." *Wendingen* 1, no. 1 (1918), p. 1.

17. W. Kromhout, "Representatief," *Bouwkunst*, 1913, p. 111.

18. In 1917 the architects' society Architectura et Amicitia (which appealed to the cultural interests of the architectural profession) was transformed into a selective group of artistically minded architects with a code of honor intended to guarantee the authorship of architectural designs. Its magazine, *Architectura*, had to be changed accordingly. In January 1918 a new magazine, *Wendingen* (Turns), appeared, with H. Th. Wijdeveld as its editor.

19. See Nic. H. M. Tummers, *J. L. Mathieu Lauweriks, Zijn werk en zijn invloed op architectuur en vormgeving rond 1910: "De Hagener Impuls"* (Hilversum: Van Saane, 1968); M. Trappeniers, "Mathieu Lauweriks als leraar in het kunstnijverheidsonderwijs," in *Nederlands Kunsthistorisch Jaarboek 1979*, v. 30 (Haarlem, 1980), pp. 173–96; Stanford Anderson, "Modern Architecture and Industry, Peter Behrens and the AEG Factories," *Oppositions*, no. 23 (1981), pp. 53–83; Alan Windsor, *Peter Behrens: Architect and Designer, 1868–1940* (New York: Whitney Library of Design, 1981), p. 55.

20. See *Amsterdamse School*, op. cit. (note 2), p. 46. For expressionism in German architecture see Marcel Franciscono, *Walter Gropius and the Creation of the Bauhaus in Weimar* (Chicago: University of Illinois Press, 1971); Wolfgang Pehnt, *Expressionist Architecture* (London: Thames and Hudson, 1973).

21. *Wendingen* was modeled after a magazine entitled *Ring*, which had been published by Lauweriks in Dusseldorf in 1908–9.

22. J. L. M. Lauweriks, "Gemeenschapskunst en Individualisme," *Wendingen* 1, no. 3 (1918), pp. 5–10.

23. Ibid., p. 7.

24. According to Lauweriks, super individualism can learn a great deal from the lower individualism of primitive people who instinctively made their utensils into art objects. This explains the interest for primitive art in *Wendingen*, where one can find articles, for example, about African sculpture, art from the Far East, and basketwork of the American Indians.

25. J. M. van der Mey, "Bouwkunst en Maatschappij," *Wendingen* 1, no. 3 (1918), pp. 3–5; idem, "Bouwkunst en Maatschappij II," *Wendingen* 1, no. 5 (1918), pp. 5–8; idem, "Bouwkunst en Maatschappij," *Wendingen* 1, no. 10 (1918), pp. 3–5.

26. J. B. van Loghem, "De Eenheid in de Komende kunst," *Wendingen* 1, no. 5 (1918), pp. 15–16.

27. C. J. Blaauw, "De Beweeglijkheid der Bouwkunst, Gemeenschapskunst en Individualisme," *Wendingen* 1, no. 6 (1918), pp. 7–12. (Quotation on p. 12.)

28. K. P. C. de Bazel, "Onze tijd en het werk van M. de Klerk," *Wendingen* 2, no. 2 (1919), pp. 3–12.

29. Ibid., p. 3.

30. J. L. M. Lauweriks, "Het Titanische in de Kunst," *Wendingen* 2, no. 4 (1919), pp. 3–5. (Quotation on p. 5.)

31. H. Th. Wijdeveld, "Inleiding" (Introduction to the Toorop issue), *Wendingen* 1, no. 12 (1918), p. 5.

32. H. Th. Wijdeveld, "Inleiding," *Wendingen* 3, nos. 3–4 (1920), p. 3.

33. How little the Amsterdam School architects were politically involved becomes clear when one considers that during the thirties some of them show sympathies for national socialism, an ideology that strove for another sort of "new world."

34. "Een kunstprogramma in Sovjet-Rusland," *Wendingen* 3, no. 1 (1920), pp. 4–10.

35. Ibid., p. 4.

36. Hardly any references to the Arts and Crafts movement are to be found in *Wendingen*. This is probably because the Amsterdam School considered the Arts and Crafts movement of the early twentieth century too advanced insofar as Ashbee, Lethaby, and others accepted the machine. Furthermore, the open ground plan typically found in the work of these English architects could not be applied in Dutch housing blocks. There are, however, many similarities between Ruskin's ideas about architecture and those of the Amsterdam School. See Kristine O. Garrigan, *Ruskin in Architecture: His Thought and His Influence* ([Madison]: University of Wisconsin Press, [1973]). Only by taking into account the relationship between the Amsterdam School and the Arts and Crafts movement will we be able to understand why the Amsterdam School was interested in the work of the American architect Frank Lloyd Wright or that of the Wiener Werkstätte architect Josef Hoffmann. These issues need further study.

37. J. L. M. Lauweriks, "Twee Hoofdrichtingen," *Wendingen* 1, no. 10 (1918), pp. 6–12. Karl Scheffler's *Der Geist der Gotik*, which also deals with this issue, was reviewed by P. H. Endt in *Wendingen* 2, no. 12 (1919), pp. 8–10.

38. H. Th. Wijdeveld, "Inleiding," *Wendingen* 4, no. 7 (1921), p. 3. For the Amsterdam School and theater see also Mansje Zijlma-Janssen, "Wendingen e il teatro," in *Wendingen 1918–1931*, op. cit. (note 2), pp. 65–69; Frans van Burkom, "Le arti monumentali in Wendingen," loc. cit., pp. 71–80.

39. Examples of this interest were clearly shown in *Wendingen*. *Wendingen* 5, nos. 8–9 (1923), is devoted to shells; in it x-rays and sections of shells are illustrated. *Wendingen* 6, nos. 11–12 (1924), is devoted to crystals.

40. H. Th. Wijdeveld, "Het Park Meerwijk," *Wendingen* 1, no. 8 (1918), p. 6.

41. The cover is on *Wendingen* 1, no. 5 (1918). Stanford Anderson describes the crystal as a symbol of the aesthetic transformation of the environment into a total work of art. See Stanford Anderson, "Peter Behrens's Changing Concept of Life as Art," *Architectural Design* 39 (February 1969), pp. 72–78. Rosemarie Bletter describes the crystal as a metaphor for social transformation by means of art. See Rosemarie Haag Bletter, "The Interpretation of the Glass Dream—Expressionist Architecture and the History of the Crystal Metaphor," *Journal of the Society of Architectural Historians* 40, no. 1 (1981), pp. 20–43.

42. A. Eibink, "De toepassing van gewapend beton," *Wendingen* 2, no. 11 (1919), p. 3.

43. For this reason, Mendelsohn's Einstein Tower near Potsdam, which was planned to be built in concrete, had to be realized in brick covered with stucco.

44. Rosemarie Haag Bletter, review of *Expressionist Architecture* by Wolfgang Pehnt, *Journal of the Society of Architectural Historians* 37 (1978), pp. 131–33.

Helen Searing

THE FORMATIVE YEARS OF MICHEL DE KLERK: INSPIRATION AND INVENTION

MORE than anyone else, Michel de Klerk was the leader and reigning genius of the Amsterdam School. Through the vitality of his buildings and the intensity of his vision, he became the inspiration for an entire generation of Dutch architects. His acknowledged masterworks, the Eigen Haard and De Dageraad housing estates, have in recent years attracted an admiration and veneration equal to that they excited when they were first erected. They are such dazzling and completely realized ensembles that one scarcely perceives the heroic efforts that lie behind their creation. De Klerk himself claimed that the act of design must be intuitive and spontaneous, yet a long and arduous apprenticeship was required before De Klerk attained such assured mastery of his own powers. For this reason, the full measure of his achievement can best be comprehended against the background of his professional development. Thanks to a solid body of surviving autograph designs that commences in 1905, this development can be exhaustively traced.

Even the most arrestingly original form-givers— and De Klerk was surely one of these—seek guidance from predecessors and contemporaries as they learn to practice their art and execute their fantasies. De Klerk found sustenance in a wide variety of formal sources, both national and foreign, familiar and exotic. Some of these sources he knew at first hand, as in the case of English Arts and Crafts design and Scandinavian vernacular and

Opposite: *Michel de Klerk. Design for a hall fireplace, 1905. Collection NDB, Amsterdam*

Eduard Cuypers. Villa at Museumplein, Amsterdam, 1905. Perspective rendering by Michel de Klerk. Collection NDB, Amsterdam

romantic architecture and, of course, the native Dutch tradition. Other influences—from the Viennese Secession, the Darmstadt Artists' Colony, and the Glasgow School—came via illustrations in books and periodicals. Sometimes the line of influence is clear, sometimes elusive.

Crucial to De Klerk's evolution as an architect was the cultural milieu of his native city, Amsterdam, during the years immediately before and after the turn of the century. A great deal of lively theoretical debate about the nature of modern architecture took place at that time in the popular and professional press and in the meetings of such organizations as Architectura et Amicitia.[1] Architectura et Amicitia in particular offered a forum for the exchange of ideas, and the lectures, evening courses, and competitions that it sponsored were important stimulants for revitalizing Dutch architecture, which had been directionless and derivative for most of the nineteenth century. The architectural philosophy expounded by such leaders of Architectura et Amicitia as Willem Kromhout and K. P. C. de Bazel would be adopted by De Klerk and the other members of the Amsterdam School, as they viewed with alarm the increasing tendency of architects to focus on technical and economic questions at the expense of aesthetics. The pursuit of *Sachlichkeit* (in Dutch, *zakelijkheid*; the word, first used in this context in Germany in the 1890s and taken over by Berlage, suggests a businesslike, efficient function-

alism) was a controversial issue in the opening decades of the twentieth century, and De Klerk took the side of those who denounced this sober, utilitarian attitude toward design.

The activities of groups like Architectura et Amicitia were especially significant for the new breed of architect that De Klerk exemplified. Born into the working class, unable to spend much time in school, this group desperately needed the opportunities for training and professional development that Architectura et Amicitia provided. Also critical to a comprehensive understanding of one's vocation is a mentor, and this De Klerk found when he encountered, in a manner almost mythical, Eduard Cuypers.

On a visit to a primary school in 1898, Cuypers noticed the fourteen-year-old De Klerk sketching a portrait. He was so impressed with the boy's drafting skills that he instantly transported the youth to the office he had set up in Amsterdam twenty years previously. The very next year, this glamorous atelier for architecture and the decorative arts would be moved to Cuypers's newly constructed house on the Jan Luykenstraat, a fine example of modern Dutch domestic design. Cuypers seems to have been unusually perspicacious in his choice of employees, for an extraordinary proportion of the budding members of the Amsterdam School passed through his office. De Klerk's fellow draftsman and future colleague, Piet Kramer, has testified how indispensable Cuypers's atelier was to his

own architectural education, although
both he and De Klerk supplemented
such on-the-job training with evening
classes at the Industrieschool voor de
Werkende Stand (Industrial School for
the Working Class).[2]

For the first years of his employment,
the teen-age De Klerk must have been
merely "the good pencil in the Master's
hand," to borrow Frank Lloyd Wright's
description of his own relationship with
Louis Sullivan. Except for a brief visit to
London in 1906, De Klerk continued to
work for Cuypers until the end of the
decade, but just after reaching his
twentieth year, he apparently felt confi-
dent enough to essay some designs on
his own. Significantly, it was precisely
at this moment that Cuypers was
beginning to retreat from the progres-
sive phase of his own practice, which
lasted from about 1898 until 1906,
toward a more conservative and historicizing approach.

One of the first designs by De Klerk
that is signed (with a monogram) and
dated (July 1905) is for a hall fireplace.
This modest project is a good starting
point for examining his evolving personal style, for it is truly a building in
embryo. Even at a time when it was
common to take the decorative arts
very seriously and to consider furniture
as micro-architecture, the sense of
solidity and plastic force that emanates
from De Klerk's proposed fireplace is
rare. In the firm, simple outlines and
the choice and treatment of materials,
the project is clearly indebted to H. P.
Berlage. This is scarcely surprising,

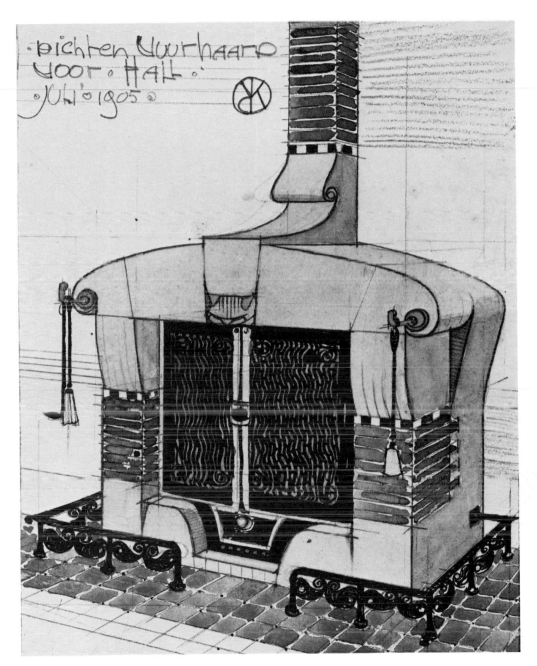

since Cuypers had already assimilated in his work features of the imposing, stone-dressed brick architecture of Berlage, who was at the height of his renown after the completion of the Amsterdam Stock Exchange in 1903.[3] As in that monumental work, so in the small fireplace the surface is kept intact and smooth, even where there is decorative embellishment and a transition from brick to stone. The extremely subtle profiling of the stone in De Klerk's design can be compared with such portions of the Stock Exchange as the exterior staircase balustrade. The sinuous rhythms of the wrought-iron trim, on the other hand, can be found in all decorative designs associated with the *Nieuwe Kunst,* the Dutch version of Art Nouveau. Indonesian art was an important component of the *Nieuwe Kunst,* and the East Indian flavor is especially prominent in furnishings produced by Cuypers's atelier.

The personalized details that give the fireplace its striking character animate De Klerk's first two architectural projects as well. One of these is a competition entry for a railroad station, known to be from 1906, the other a design for a garage, which probably dates from the same year.[4] Both are Berlagian in that they are conceived in terms of brick with stone trim kept flush with the taut wall surfaces, but now another influence can be discerned, that of late Victorian/Edwardian architecture. This circumstance suggests that the drawings were made after De Klerk's abortive trip to England

to seek employment, although Cuypers's residential design of this period also displayed many affinities with the Queen Anne style (see page 68). In any case, contemporary English practice was especially appropriate to the Netherlands, for the British architects who revived the Baroque and Queen Anne modes were using forms that had their origin in Dutch architecture of the sixteenth and early seventeenth centuries.

Thus, the bull's-eye windows of the garage, the silhouette and ornamentation of the gable of the railroad station, and the distribution and articulation of the fenestration in both projects reveal the impact of English architecture, directly or at second hand. Furthermore, the exuberance and richness of the imagery contrasts strikingly with the sobriety displayed by Berlage and his followers. The buildings that De Klerk may have seen in London[5] could have led him in this direction, but so could his training under Cuypers, who disdained the extreme abnegation that was fashionable among many Dutch architects.

Of the three competition entries that the ambitious young draftsman prepared in 1907, the one for a row house in Amsterdam, for a competition sponsored by the weekly paper *De Groene Amsterdammer,* is closest to the projects of the previous year in its materials and composition. However, it is a more restrained and mature design, based on the traditional Amsterdam town house. The brick patterns that outline the

Opposite: Michel de Klerk. Competition design for a railroad station, 1906. Elevation and plan. Collection NDB, Amsterdam

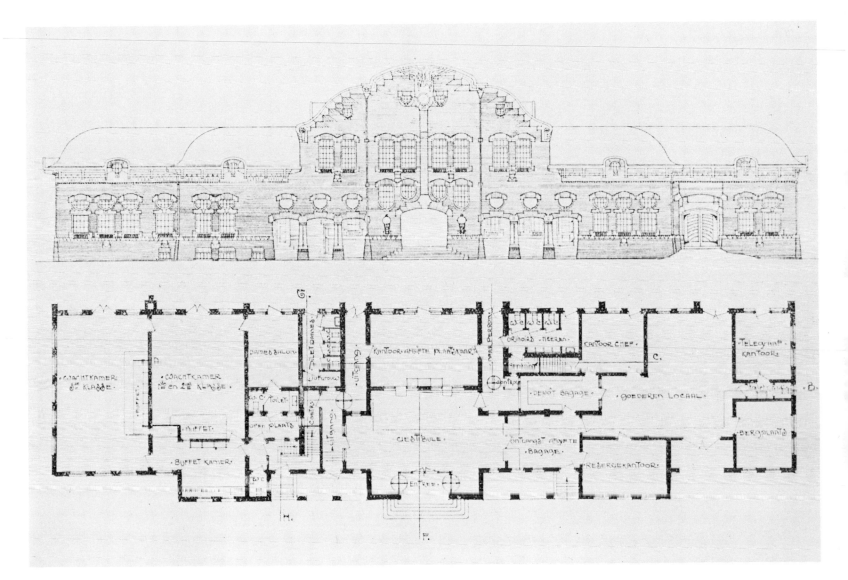

edges of the gable had already appeared in the design for the garage; such a treatment is paralleled not only in Dutch architecture of the period but also in Danish work. Despite the conventional *parti*, the upper portion of the facade is novel in its proportions and contours. The shallow, pedimental form over the trio of windows looks forward to Hillehuis (see pages 88–89), as does the division of the lower wall by piers. Although there is no evidence that De Klerk at this point knew the work of Frank Lloyd Wright (1869–1959),[6] the alternation of piers and windows is very Wrightian, as is the emphasis on the horizontal courses of brick.

For the row house, his most straightforward design of the period, De Klerk was awarded first prize, although he had to share this with two other entrants. The latter were commended because their projects, although not artistically pleasing, could be built for the stated sum; De Klerk's design was chosen for the commodious handling of space and for its aesthetic qualities. Kramer received second prize, but he too was required to share it with a more functionally oriented competitor.

The lack of a clear-cut decision may reflect the makeup of the five-man jury. Three of the four architect members—Berlage, Kromhout, and Johannes Verheul (1860–1948)[7]—had been exponents of the *Nieuwe Kunst*, but while Kromhout and Verheul remained faithful to the general principles of that movement, Berlage had rejected its concern with decoration. The fourth architect, J. H. W. Leliman (1879–1921),

Opposite: *Michel de Klerk. Competition design for a row house, motto* Grasmaand *("Grass Month" [April]), 1907. Perspective. Collection NDB, Amsterdam*

Michel de Klerk. Design for a garage, 1906 (?). Collection NDB, Amsterdam

practiced in a traditional style and also wrote architectural history. He was the editor of *De Bouwwereld* from its founding in 1902 until his death; in that capacity, he would prove a hostile critic to De Klerk and the work of the emerging Amsterdam School.[8] The fifth juror was the civil engineer J. W. C. Tellegen (1859–1921), who played a major role in shaping the liberal housing policy of Amsterdam, an interesting connection in view of De Klerk's eventual involvement with that policy. Tellegen had been responsible for formulating the

municipality's strict building code of 1905; for the last seven years of his life he served as Amsterdam's mayor.

The two other projects of this year were made for competitions sponsored by Bouwkunst en Vriendschap (Architecture and Friendship), the Rotterdam counterpart of Amsterdam's Architectura et Amicitia. De Klerk took the opportunity to experiment with hitherto untried building materials—wood for the clubhouse for an athletic field and reinforced concrete for the café-restaurant, to which he gave the cunning

motto *Monoliet* (Monolith). More unusual in materials, they are also more bizarre in detailing. De Klerk nonetheless received a second prize for each, from a less distinguished jury.

The clubhouse bears a striking resemblance to late-nineteenth-century American domestic architecture in its massing and in the specification of horizontal wooden siding, a material used far less widely in the Netherlands than in the United States, although one can find houses in some of the little fishing villages, such as Marken, near

House on Crescent Street, Northampton, Mass.

Amsterdam, that are clad in wood. As in his previous designs in brick, De Klerk created two-dimensional patterns integral with the building material by cutting the wooden clapboards into odd shapes for decorative ends. Apparently, De Klerk thought wood peculiarly appropriate to sporting functions; he used horizontal wooden siding for the rowing club De Hoop, one of the last commissions completed before his death.

The picturesque massing disguises the formality of the plan, which also has a curiously American character. The organization of the spaces, with the dining room extending outward from the central mass toward the veranda, is reminiscent of the compositions of

Wright; here, the buffet replaces the fireplace as core. The similarity may lie only in a common source, such as the Japanese pavilion,[9] but it is rather tantalizing. There is no precedent for such a plan in Cuypers's work.

The most quirky design of all was for the café-restaurant. The round windows of the garage and railroad station appear in combination with the same oddly shaped openings as are found in the clubhouse. The jury criticized the project on functional grounds, citing an unsatisfactory connection between the main space and the billiard room. The report also commented that the many projections and recessions led to a confusing impression of the whole, but acknowledged that "the facade is not

without charm, though somewhat forced and clearly influenced by the modern German conception."[10]

By "the modern German conception," the jurors presumably meant *Jugendstil*, and perhaps even more specifically, the work of the Austrian Joseph Maria Olbrich (1867–1908).[11] Trained by Otto Wagner (1841–1918), and a member of the Viennese Secession, Olbrich in 1899 moved to Darmstadt as a member of and chief architect to the Künstler-Kolonie (Artists' Colony) founded there by Ernst Ludwig, Grand Duke of Hesse. He would remain in Darmstadt until his untimely death of leukemia at the age of forty, just one year older than De Klerk would be when his brilliant career likewise was

Opposite, right: *Michel de Klerk. Competition design for a clubhouse, motto de 4de (The Fourth [competition]), 1907. Perspective. Collection NDB, Amsterdam.* Color page 20. Below: *Plan*

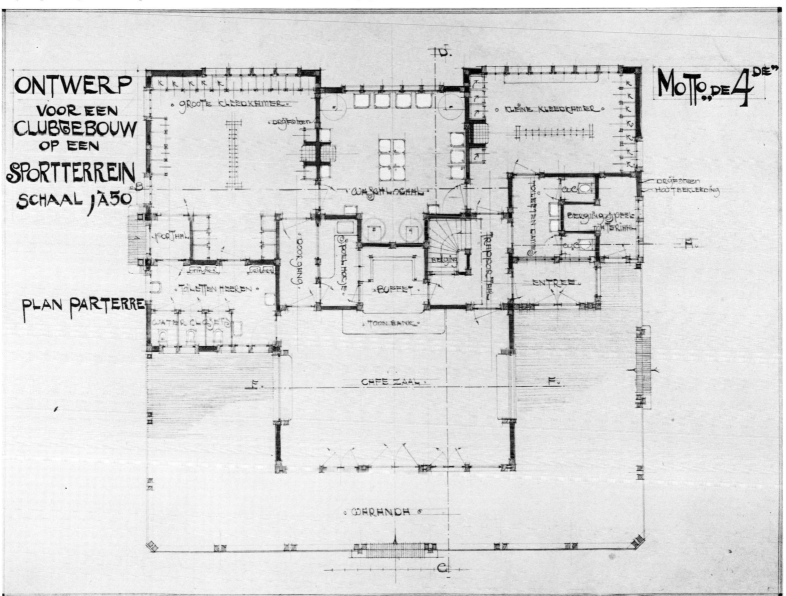

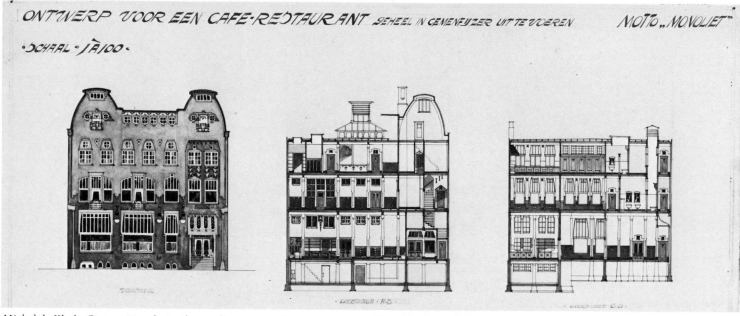

Michel de Klerk. Competition design for a café-restaurant in concrete, motto Monoliet (Monolith), *1907. Perspective and sections. Collection NDB, Amsterdam*

tragically terminated.

Olbrich's work was widely published, and the buildings that he designed for the Künstler-Kolonie on the Mathildenhöhe were full of touches that De Klerk evidently admired. In addition to borrowing specific motifs, such as the stylized gambrel shape (see pages 88–89), he learned from Olbrich how to transform the familiar into the piquant. De Klerk's technique of truncation—as in the asymmetrical gables of the clubhouse, and the parabola-shaped windows of both the clubhouse and the restaurant—may have been an operation derived from Olbrich, who had sliced off the top of triangular windows in his exhibition theater at Darmstadt of 1900–1901. The wooden posts of that

building foreshadow those of the clubhouse veranda, and the mansarded tower found on De Klerk's structure may have had its origin in Olbrich's Deiters house of 1900–1901; De Klerk also patterned his lettering on that of Olbrich.

But Olbrich was very much an architect of the previous generation, interested in the two-dimensional ornamental possibilities of his craft, whereas in De Klerk's work, the distinction between two-dimensional decoration and three-dimensional construction has been dissolved. De Klerk's ornament is not applied, as was so much of Olbrich's, but grows from the fabric of the building, and the eye-catching details of his mature work are fully integrated

with the whole conception rather than existing separately. Much of Olbrich's work was stuccoed, and this tended to reinforce the surficial nature of the embellishment. Olbrich, like the other Viennese masters of the Secession movement, came from a background in which classicism had been dominant, and it is this Hellenic component that gives the Austrian variant of Art Nouveau its special flavor. Classicism and its underlying rationality held no appeal for De Klerk. However, both men responded very positively to vernacular buildings, and Olbrich tempered the extravagant bourgeois individuality of his houses at Darmstadt by introducing elements derived from peasant architecture.

In praising the clubhouse design, the jury had nonetheless warned that:

> perhaps it is more decorative than architectonic. The designer has sought picturesque solutions which harm the coherence of the whole. …The capping of the tower is weak and unattractive, the window openings impractical and ugly.[12]

Possibly such commentary persuaded De Klerk to take a less controversial and subjective approach in the next competition he entered, for a group of four workers' dwellings, in 1908. In fact, the program itself, which was quite restrictive, may have pushed him in the same direction (see pages 80-81).

This was De Klerk's first venture into workers' housing, the building type that would become his major field of accomplishment. Since the project was for a one-and-a-half story, four-family row house on the "outskirts of a provincial city," it was somewhat different in nature from the four-story urban blocks that would dominate his energies after he set up independent practice in 1911, but the gusto and thoroughness with which he tackled the program were prophetic. His plans are much more intricate than those published in the booklet of approved entries;[13] there are more internal partitions, for example, making for greater privacy and intimacy, if perhaps also for more expense. Further, De Klerk provided two different layouts for each pair of

Joseph Maria Olbrich. Julius Glückert house, Darmstadt, 1900–1901. Rear view. From Architektur von Olbrich, *vol. 1, by Joseph M. Olbrich (Berlin, 1901), plate 55*

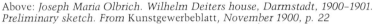

Above: *Joseph Maria Olbrich. Wilhelm Deiters house, Darmstadt, 1900–1901. Preliminary sketch. From* Kunstgewerbeblatt, *November 1900, p. 22*

Below: *Joseph Maria Olbrich. Exhibition theater, Darmstadt, 1900–1901. From* Architektur von Olbrich, *vol. 1, by Joseph M. Olbrich (Berlin, 1901), plate 47*

dwellings, something virtually no other contestant took the time to do.

The tight budget doubtless accounts for the relatively self-effacing elevations and tame details. Nevertheless, the treatment of the upper story is rather unconventional. The bull's-eye windows might be criticized on pragmatic grounds, for they would hardly have provided sufficient light to the master bedroom; this was not the first time that De Klerk placed formal effects before practical requirements, nor would it be the last. Still, it is clear that he pondered carefully the urbanistic challenge of reproducing the project in a series, for he has invented a dynamic method of visually linking the units. Unlike the central pair of gables, the end gables—truncated, asymmetrical—look incomplete on their own. However, had the four-family units been repeated along the length of a street, this tactic would have activated the space between with a lively sense of tension. This rather Mannerist ploy would be typical of De Klerk's future design strategies.

Although the terms of the competition did not require it, De Klerk made a perspective sketch of the proposed living room. The window seat, exposed beams, and sturdy built-in furniture betray his admiration for the Arts and Crafts movement in Britain and possibly the United States; there is a resemblance to the work of Gustav Stickley (1858–1942), for example. The use of a continuous horizontal band under the ceiling recalls the practice of Wright and

Charles Rennie Mackintosh (1868–1928), both of whom had learned this device from their study of Japanese interiors.

Also indebted to English Arts and Crafts architecture is the treatment of the upper facade, with its plastered surfaces and circular windows, and one historian has pointed out the possible influence of C. R. Ashbee (1863–1942).[14] In addition, memories of Olbrich's work at Darmstadt are stirred by the blunted shapes that frame voids and recessions. Ultimately, De Klerk transcended his sources. Although this design remains unresolved, it gave him the opportunity to test certain design techniques that would be perfected at a later date. Thus, the rhythmic rise and fall of the massing and the insertion of a terrace into the upper part of the facade anticipate his De Dageraad housing on the Pieter Lodewijk Takstraat (see page 48).

Two alternate schemes of 1909 for a country house were not prompted by a competition, and perhaps a commission had been in the offing. One of these, crisply rendered in pen and ink, resembles the workers' dwellings of the previous year, with its curious windows and its use of stucco over brick. The variant country house design, sketchily presented in soft pencil, has a thatched roof, conventional dormers, and a lower story of exposed brick topped by wooden siding; it is not unlike the simple rural houses designed by De Bazel and Cuypers during the 1900s, which have thatched roofs and a vernacular char-

Michel de Klerk. Two designs for a two-family country house, 1909. Collection NDB, Amsterdam. Above: *Ink rendering;* below: *pencil rendering*

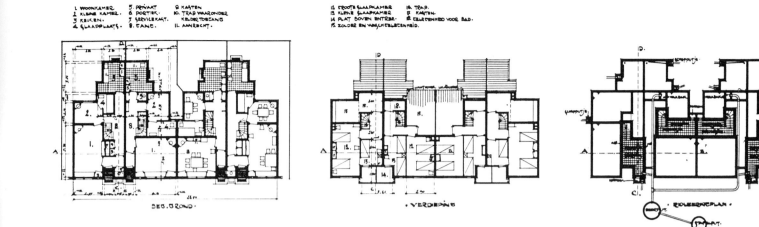

Michel de Klerk. Competition design for a block of four workers' dwellings, motto Het Beloofde Land (The Promised Land), 1908. Collection NDB, Amsterdam. Top: Plan; above: perspective; opposite: perspective of living room

HET BELOOFDE LAND

acter. The design of the chimney, which rises from an arch sliced off at one side, pays homage to Berlage, who had used such a detail in his Villa Parkwijk of 1900, a building De Klerk admired. The distribution of spaces in the two versions of the country house seems identical, and both are shown enclosed by a low wall that is similar in treatment to the fireplace design of 1905 (see page 69).

In 1910, De Klerk may be said to have triumphantly come of age. He married, left Cuypers's employ, made a trip to Scandinavia, and designed a competition entry that is uniquely his own, which marked him as a young architect to be watched. Shortly after De Klerk's death, the critic J. P. Mieras recalled the stunning impact of this design, claiming that "there was latent in it an entirely new expression in architecture."[15] Nevertheless, the jury, which included Kromhout, De Bazel, and Leliman, described the project in terms that subsequently would be repeated with regard to De Klerk's total oeuvre:

> in general, the construction is decorative, the decoration constructive, and in both there dominates an exaggeration which harms the total conception.[16]

Despite this equivocal judgment, De Klerk received the cash award set aside for the second prize, though the honor of the prize itself was withheld.

This competition, which was sponsored by Bouwkunst en Vriendschap,

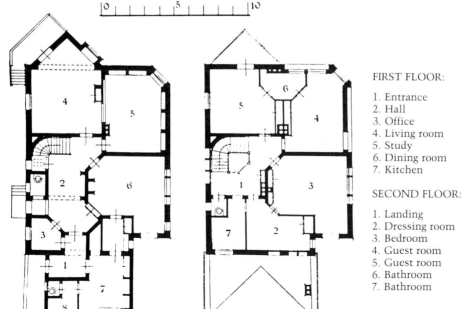

FIRST FLOOR:

1. Entrance
2. Hall
3. Office
4. Living room
5. Study
6. Dining room
7. Kitchen

SECOND FLOOR:

1. Landing
2. Dressing room
3. Bedroom
4. Guest room
5. Guest room
6. Bathroom
7. Bathroom

H. P. Berlage. Villa Parkwijk, Amsterdam, 1900. Photograph, Collection NDB, Amsterdam.
Above: *Ground plan*

was for a

nondenominational cemetery
for a large city, with a
monumental entrance,
service buildings, and a
mortuary chapel. The chapel
must dominate the complex
and have a character worthy
of its high and serious
purpose.[17]

Such an ambitious program provided the challenge necessary to spur De Klerk on toward a more original and controlled idiom than he had achieved heretofore.

It should be noted that some of the drawings are composed over a grid of diamonds and squares. This is the earliest evidence that De Klerk was familiar with an important design procedure that had developed in the last decade of the nineteenth century among the most advanced Dutch architects, and it introduces the vital subject of the role of proportional systems in Dutch architecture. Berlage had used a geometric system in the Amsterdam Stock Exchange, which was probably the first realized example of its employment, but he made no claim to have invented it. Rather, he acknowledged that De Bazel, J. L. M. Lauweriks, and the theoretician and teacher J. H. de Groot (1865–1932) had been the originators in modern times of this method. The use in medieval times of triangulation and quadrature, on which the Dutch proportional systems were based, had been described in the publications of the influential Eugène Emmanuel Viollet-le-Duc (1814–79), widely read in the Netherlands.[18]

De Klerk could have learned about proportional systems in the series of evening lectures, called by the theosophically inspired name Vahânacursus,[19] that were given by De Bazel and Lauweriks at Architectura et Amicitia, or he could have read about them in the writings of Berlage and De Groot. It is possible that his knowledge that De Bazel was on the jury prompted him to use such a method. The mortuary nature of the program may also have been a factor in its employment. De Bazel and Lauweriks believed that the ancient Egyptians, the preeminent masters of funerary architecture, had used geometric systems to instill a cosmic harmony and divine inevitability that brought these works an appropriate sense of permanence.

De Klerk chose to employ a dual network of regulating lines. Within each square are four isosceles triangles joined to make a diamond-patterned grid. The dimensions of the various buildings are determined by the squares —the proportions of the mortuary

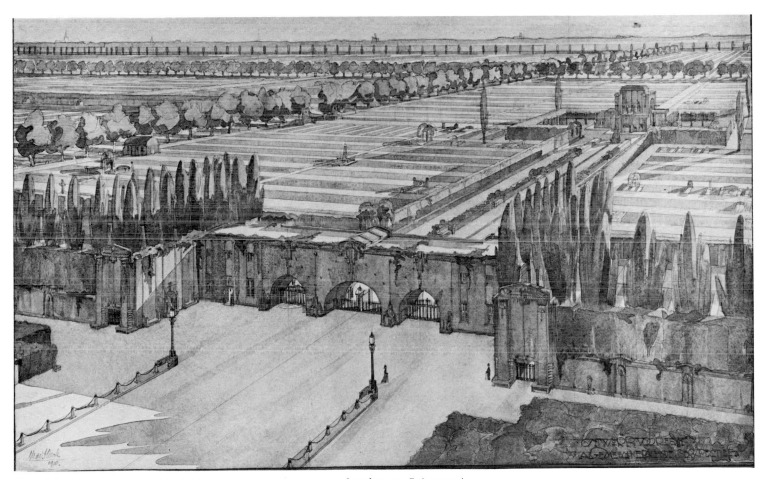

Michel de Klerk. Competition design for a cemetery with mortuary chapel, motto Reincarnatie *(Reincarnation), 1910. Bird's-eye view of cemetery from main entrance. Collection NDB, Amsterdam*

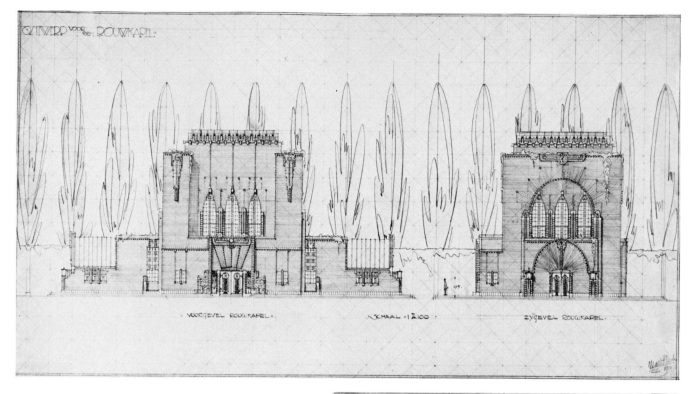

Michel de Klerk. Mortuary chapel. Collection NDB, Amsterdam. Opposite, above: *Elevations;* opposite, below: *perspective.* Color page 17.   Above: *detail of entrance*

chapel proper, for example, are five by six by seven, the kind of progression often encountered when geometric systems are used. The width of the side elevation is five units (six with its projecting entrance), the front elevation is six units (sixteen with the lower wings of the waiting rooms, which are two-and-a-half units high), and the height of the chapel is seven units. Entrances, windows, and ornamental details are disposed and proportioned in accordance with the intersections of the triangles. The width of the doors is equal to the hypotenuse of one isosceles triangle, and the paraboloid windows, two units in height, are centered within the diamond-shaped grid.[20]

De Bazel's and Lauweriks's influences on this design may go beyond the use of a geometric system. The figurative sculpture flanking the main entrance has that hieratic, Symbolist character found in De Bazel's decorative designs of the late 1890s. These forbidding and brooding images, including the heads in the stained-glass windows above the door, also resemble figures in the painting *Evolution* by Piet Mondrian (1872–1944). Like De Bazel and Lauweriks, Mondrian was a theosophist, and although De Klerk was not a member of this quasi-philosophical, quasi-religious sect, in which Occidental rationalism was tempered by Eastern mysticism, his friends belonging to the theosophical circle in Amsterdam must have acquainted him with their beliefs.[21]

The taste for the exotic that the

Nieuwe Kunst brought to Dutch architecture has already been cited, and survives very strongly in De Klerk's project. Coexisting with such Dutch elements as Indonesian motifs and proportional systems, however, are lingering traces of Viennese influence. The monumentality of the massing, the academic discipline that informs the composition, and the relations of the main chapel to the barrel-vaulted waiting rooms bring to mind the works of Otto Wagner and his followers. But no Viennese architect would have employed such lavish terra-cotta details, nor constructed his building of the specially formed purplish red bricks that De Klerk envisaged. That such extravagant ornament could in fact be executed precisely according to the architect's specifications would be demonstrated with the Scheepvaarthuis of 1912-16, a stunning building on which De Klerk and Kramer collaborated under the direction of Johan van der Mey.

Eye-catching as the detail of the chapel is, one cannot agree with the jury that it tends to overpower the architectonic force of the building. For the first time, De Klerk fully mastered the problem of designing in the round and related the plastic forms to one another with three-dimensional clarity. Berlage had provided an example of tectonic monumentality in his Stock Exchange, but had been very sparing in his use of ornament. In contrast, Kromhout's American Hotel of 1898-1901, which, incidentally, was designed on the basis of a geometric grid, is far closer in spirit

to De Klerk's work. Indeed, De Klerk may have learned from Kromhout how to play off judiciously the small details against the larger mass.

In December 1910, when he was notified of the jury's decision to award him a cash prize, De Klerk was in Stockholm. One may inquire why De Klerk chose to visit Denmark and Sweden. There is evidence of a lively interest in Scandinavian architecture among members of his generation. Van der Mey went to Copenhagen in 1906 with the proceeds of his Prix de Rome, and Dutch architectural magazines regularly chronicled building activities in Scandinavia. The architectural ties between the Netherlands and the Nordic countries had been forged long before, and many of the great monuments of the Northern Renaissance in Denmark and Sweden had been designed and executed by Netherlanders. Another Dutch architect sojourning in Denmark around the time of De Klerk's visit, D. F. Slothouwer (1884-?), made use of his stay to write *Bouwkunst der Nederlandsche renaissance in Denemarken.*[22]

Since there is no written record of De Klerk's opinions of Danish architecture, it may be useful to interpolate some of Slothouwer's observations. He found Danish buildings marked by a strong striving after individuality, with each architect conspicuously seeking markedly personal forms, so much so that at the beginning of his stay he had no clear picture of a national architecture. On further acquaintance, he perceived something of a national style emerging, which utilized older traditions while

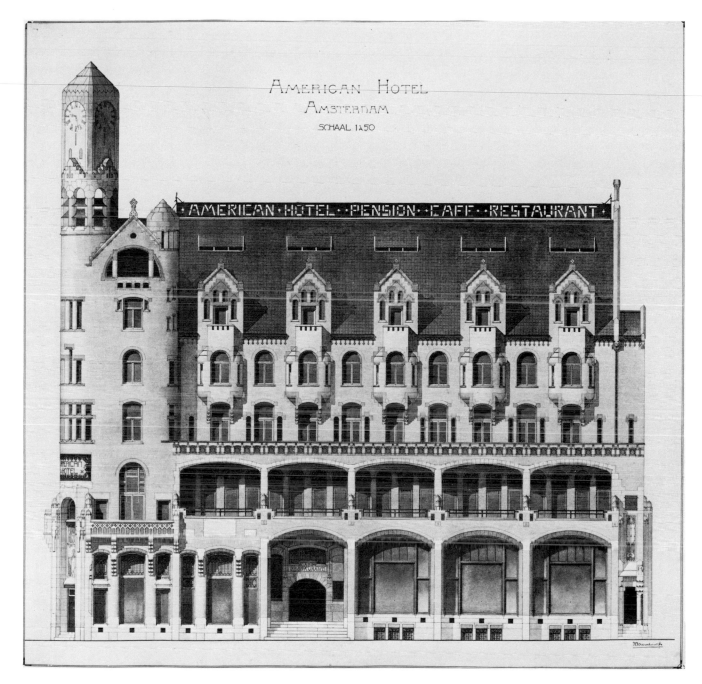

offering something new and adventurous.[23] It is significant that it was the strong originality of early twentieth-century Danish design that so impressed Slothouwer, and one can posit that De Klerk, who was his exact contemporary, shared some of his reactions.

De Klerk did document his journey in a glowing series of travel sketches. In Sweden, most of his drawings depicted the old buildings brought from all over Scandinavia to the open-air museum at Skansen. He apparently loved the rough shingled and wooden textures of the vernacular architecture of country villages and farms, the vivid plastic shapes of houses and clock towers, and the snug rooms whose sturdy design

may have seemed a simpler version of the interiors produced in Cuypers's office. In Denmark he sketched both sixteenth- and seventeenth-century buildings near Copenhagen, and such examples of National Romanticism as the town hall (1892–1905) by Martin Nyrop (1849–1921) and the newly completed Palads Hotel (1907–10) by Anton Rosen (1859–1928). Always, De Klerk sought the picturesque and the piquant, and memories of his Scandinavian journey would enrich the wealthy store of forceful visual images for which he became noted.

De Klerk returned in 1911 to his first independent commission. This was for a block of middle-class flats on the

Johannes Vermeerplein, part of the area near the Rijksmuseum that had been laid out at the end of the nineteenth century for an urban development that catered to the well-to-do. The clients, G. Kamphuis and Klaas Hille, were contractors, and the building, usually called Hillehuis, was ready in 1912.

The design as a whole does not greatly affront the sobriety of mainstream Dutch architecture of the period, unlike De Klerk's subsequent commissions. Hillehuis is much more restrained, for example, than the next building he would execute for Hille, the block of workers' dwellings on the Spaarndammerplantsoen. Nevertheless, De Klerk's authorship is instantly recognizable in

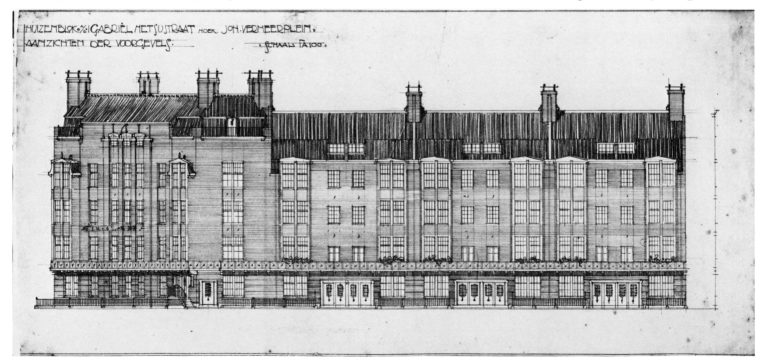

Michel de Klerk. Housing block, Hillehuis, on the Johannes Vermeerplein, 1911. Opposite: *Elevation on Metsustraat and Vermeerplein.*
Collection NDB, Amsterdam

the unusual details and the rhythmic composition.

The fenestration has not been conceived in the repetitive manner of most apartment houses of the time, but has been organized to present a series of major and minor accents to enliven the facades. The portion of the elevation facing the square (the Johannes Vermeerplein) makes the most dramatic statement. Double bay windows, capped by De Klerk's beloved gambrel shape, frame a central trio of sash set within projecting vertical piers. The piers are joined at the top by shieldlike forms resembling those on the main facade of the mortuary chapel; they carry the legend Anno Domini MCMXII. The windows are flush with the wall plane rather than set back to reveal the depth of the bearing structure; this visual continuity of surface was to become a characteristic feature of De Klerk's housing designs. The treatment of the tiled roof is also revelatory of De Klerk's personal style: a conventional mansard has been transformed into a more flowing and striking termination.

In Hillehuis, De Klerk demonstrated that the dazzling effects conveyed by his drawings could be translated accurately into architecture. Flat and low-relief patterns enrich the walls and balconies in a way that does not repudiate the then-current demand for truth to materials and integration of ornament and construction. The carved designs on the stone corbels, the grilles of the doors, and the ironwork of the fence are three-dimensional versions of the angular graphic designs created by artists associated with the *Nieuwe Kunst*.

The commission for Hillehuis ini-tiated De Klerk's private practice, and he came through with flying colors. By 1915, at the sixtieth anniversary exhibition of Architectura et Amicitia, his renderings would be hung in the Salon of Honor (*eerezaal*), beside those of Berlage and De Bazel. During the eight years he had remaining, he would become an architectural legend.

From his first independent efforts, De Klerk's work was distinguished by its subjective lyricism. In love with the poetic potentiality of architectural form, he avidly devoured images that moved and excited him as he learned to create his own expressive forms. The fertility of his imagination led him toward individualistic but accessible formal inventions, which in turn became a source of inspiration for his peers and his followers in the Amsterdam School.

Michel de Klerk. First block on the Spaarndammerplantsoen, Amsterdam, 1913-14. Perspective. Collection NDB, Amsterdam. Color pages 18-19

NOTES

1. Architectura et Amicitia was founded in 1855. Published under its aegis at various times were *De Opmerker* (1883–92), *De Bouwmeester* (1884–95), *De Architect* (1890–1918), and *Architectura* (1893–1915; 1921–26), as well as *Wendingen* (1918–31). Its motto, *Place aux Jeunes*, made it a more attractive organization to a figure like De Klerk than the oldest Dutch architectural society, a national association with local chapters, the Maatschappij tot Bevordering der Bouwkunst (Society for the Encouragement of Architecture), established in 1842. Both groups pursued parallel activities, though Architectura et Amicitia was more oriented toward architecture as an art than as a lucrative profession. The Maatschappij tot Bevordering der Bouwkunst published *Bouwkundige Bijdragen* (1842–81), *Bouwkundig Weekblad* (1881–1926), and *Bouwkundig Tijdschrift* (1881–1908).

2. B. W. Wierink was singled out as a particularly important teacher at this evening school by De Klerk and Kramer. Wierink had been a pupil of P. J. H. Cuypers (1827–1921), an important Dutch Gothic Revival architect who had concerned himself with reviving the crafts in the Netherlands after the example of William Morris.

3. For superb illustrations as well as an exemplary analysis of the Stock Exchange, see P. Singelenberg, *H. P. Berlage, Idea and Style* (Utrecht: Haentjens, Dekker, and Gumbert, 1972).

4. These two projects are discussed and illustrated in H. Searing, "Berlage or Cuypers? The Father of Them All" (see Bibliography).

5. For good pictorial coverage of the buildings that De Klerk may have seen on his London trip, see especially Alastair Service, *London, 1900* (New York: Rizzoli International, 1979) and Peter Davey, *Architecture of the Arts and Crafts Movement* (London and New York: Rizzoli International, 1980).

6. Frank Lloyd Wright's impact on Dutch architecture has been thoroughly surveyed in the catalogue *Americana* (Otterlo: Rijksmuseum Kröller-Müller, 1975), pp. 20–24, 28–40. Wright's work was known in Europe from 1910, generally via the Wasmuth publications, and in Holland, particularly via lectures by Berlage, who had visited the United States in 1911. But were illustrations of Wright's work available before this date? Leonard Eaton, in *American Architecture Comes of Age* (Cambridge, Mass.: The MIT Press, 1972), p. 208, relates that the Prairie School architect William Gray Purcell "recalled that Berlage was well-informed about [Wright and] had studied [his] work." If periodicals discussing Wright's work were available in the Netherlands to Berlage, perhaps they were to De Klerk as well.

7. For Verheul, see A. Voogd, ed., *J. Verheul, Dzn. Architect—Rotterdam* (Bussum: Gustav Schueler, 1916) and J. Roding, *'De Utrecht' een Nederlands voorbeeld van Art-Nouveau-architectuur* (Utrecht: Het Spectrum, 1972).

8. When it emerged that the list of suitable architects to be employed on designing publicly supported workers' housing consisted primarily of members of the Amsterdam School, Leliman opposed it *(De Bouwwereld* 16 (1917), pp. 57–59, 89–92). He attacked the composition of the Amsterdam Schoonheidscommissie (Committee for Aesthetic Advice) when it became dominated by architects sympathetic to the Amsterdam School:

   > Until seven years ago the Amsterdam *Schoonheidscommissie* consisted of well-known architects who had won their spurs and were on guard against being too rigorous. But since the young people got hold of it, with their rashness as well as their ideals, the commission has become a powerful influence, marked by conflicts and clashes....

   De Bouwwereld 20 (1921), p. 82.

9. The plans of Frank Lloyd Wright that De Klerk's plan resembles include the Martin house of 1904 and the Bok house of 1906. Architects associated with De Stijl—Rob van 't Hoff and Jan Wils—would also utilize this type of plan as a starting point, as would C. J. Blaauw of the Amsterdam School, in a house at Park Meerwijk. Wright apparently derived it from the Hoo-o-den Pavilion erected at the World's Columbian Exposition in Chicago in 1893.

10. *Bouwkundig Weekblad* 27 (1907), p. 809.

11. For Olbrich, see the lavishly illustrated book

by Ian Latham, *Joseph Maria Olbrich* (New York: Rizzoli International, 1980).

12. *Bouwkundig Weekblad* 27 (1907), p. 809.

13. *Eengezins-werkmanswoningen* (The Hague: Mouton and Co., 1908). The competition was sponsored by the Maatschappij tot Bevordering der Bouwkunst (see note 1), which selected 40 of the 230 entries for inclusion in this booklet. Those illustrated are more utilitarian than De Klerk's entry. One of the projects, however, did have bull's-eye windows like those found in De Klerk's design. Interestingly, it was the entry of B. van der Nieuwer-Amstel, one of the architects whose name would appear on the approved list referred to in note 8. He would design facades for the dwellings constructed around the Vrijheidslaan in Amsterdam-South by a consortium of private builders, Amstels Bouw Vereeniging. The jury for this competition consisted of two minor architects who were public health inspectors, two who directed municipal public works, and Leliman.

14. Suzanne S. Frank, "Michel de Klerk (1884–1923): An Architect of the Amsterdam School" (see Bibliography), chapter 5.

15. J. P. Mieras, *Bouwkundig Weekblad* 45 (1924), p. 111.

16. Quoted in *Wonen-TA/BK*, no. 19 (1973), p. 21.

17. *De Bouwwereld* 9 (1910), pp. 267–68.

18. A very thorough discussion of proportional systems, in Dutch, is to be found in A. W. Reinink, *K. P. C. de Bazel, Architect* (Leiden: Universitaire Pers, 1965); this has been summarized in my dissertation (see Bibliography). Reyner Banham, *Theory and Design in the First Machine Age* (London: The Architectural Press, 1960), provides a useful consideration in English of this issue.

19. The course was named after the Vahâna-Lodge, a branch of the Theosophical Society established in 1896 by De Bazel and Lauweriks. The course, which met on Friday evenings in the headquarters of Architectura et Amicitia, consisted of theoretical instruction in descriptive geometry and practical training in technique and in the application of geometric systems to aesthetics and art history. (Ernst Braches, *Het boek als Nieuwe Kunst, Een Studie in Art Nouveau* [Utrecht: Oosthoek, 1973], p. 113). The course was given from 1897 to 1902. *Vahâna* is Sanskrit for "conveyance" or "vehicle" (*voertuig*) (M. Bok, *Architectura* [Amsterdam: Stichting Architectuurmuseum, 1975], p. 94).

20. The parabola evidently had a particular meaning in the context of this program. J. C. Slebos, in *Grondslagen voor aesthetiek en stijl (Fundamentals of aesthetics and style*; Amsterdam: J. Ahrend, 1939), p. 126, considered the parabola to be particularly suitable for a *memento mori*, because "it is an ellipse of which the second focus moves to infinity. It is thus part of the infinite. The parabola is preeminently suitable as an element for the monument." One is reminded of the belief of Antonio Gaudi, whose work shows so many affinities with that of De Klerk (though no direct connection between the two has ever been established), that the parabola symbolized the Trinity. Slebos's book was a belated argument in favor of using proportional systems. He illustrated one of De Klerk's drawings for the chapel as evidence that a system of diamonds and squares is "nowadays [!] applied by many prominent architects."

21. Suzanne Frank, op. cit. (note 14), pp. 101-2, has pointed out that De Klerk's motto for this entry, *Reincarnatie* (Reincarnation), has a theosophical ring to it. To my knowledge, there is no useful consideration in English of the impact of theosophy on Dutch architecture.

22. Published in Amsterdam in 1924.

23. Sven Risom, "Holland" (interview with Slothouwer), *Architekten* 16 (1911), pp. 185–87.

Maristella Casciato

To a friend of the light
If you don't want to weaken your senses
and your eyes,
you can still chase after the sun, but in
the shade.

Friedrich Nietzsche, no. 12, "Jest, Malice
and Vengeance," *The Gay Science*

MICHEL DE KLERK: UTOPIA BUILT

As an architect, Michel de Klerk was preeminently a builder. He rarely drew architectural fantasies; those he did had the qualities of true exercises that confront the insidious problems connected with construction. He did not write but let his architecture speak for him. It seems paradoxical, when discussing an architect so devoted to the cult of construction and to maintaining logic from the first sketch to the final project, to talk of utopia. Yet, not only in his drawings, but above all in his constructions, an inner force of utopian ideal was felt from the very beginning. This will be analyzed, also in relation to the presumed links that have been established between De Klerk and that forge of utopias that was the composite phenomenon called German Expressionism.[1]

The tenacious plant that was the Amsterdam School appeared and grew to its maximum splendor in the span of about ten years, between 1914 and 1923. At first it looked like the solitary tree of pure individuality, but the species had deep roots in the Dutch soil, and it quickly spread beyond the national boundaries. Its fruit was an architecture so plastic that it looked like sculpture

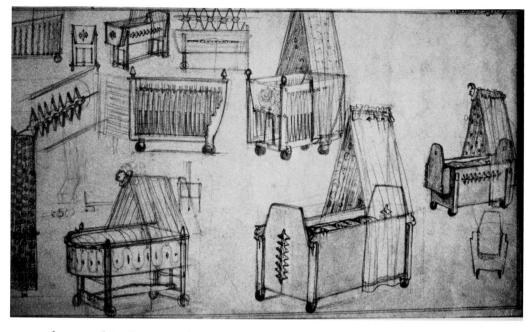

Michel de Klerk. Sketches of a crib, October 1912. Collection NDB, Amsterdam

Opposite: *Michel de Klerk. Sketch of old Stockholm, January 1911. Pencil and crayon. Collection NDB, Amsterdam*

and so graphic that it simulated painting.

De Klerk was so involved with this original conception of architecture that he was actually identified with it. He was its inspirer as well as its most open-minded interpreter. He exalted its absolute imagery, but always brought it back into the human dimension. He breathed the spirit of fantasy into the rational process of generating architecture, and he did so with a vitality comparable to that emanating from Nietzsche's *Gay Science.* The poet of the "sparkling new," the "sensationally shocking"[2]—as De Klerk himself defined his work and that of his friends in those early years—was an individual of exceptional qualities, well suited to a *science* that was indeed *gay,* and whose

character differed so much from the *seriousness* customary with "the study of average behavior, the search of norms, and the cautious formulation of hypotheses."[3]

As in the case of the "friend of the light," neither doubt nor uncertainty was absent from this *habitus.* However, this is exactly the meaning of Nietzsche's "gay science": to recognize oneself as an active principle of an existence accepted with all its contradictions.[4] From this derived that special detachment that led De Klerk to the discovery of a rational and daily imagery that does not oppress or suppress art (and architecture), something like a "utopia of meaning."

His friend and collaborator Piet Kramer said of De Klerk, "The power of conviction that radiates from his drawings gives us that curious, happy feeling of being closer and closer to the Almighty."[5] Certainly the luminosity of his architectural drawings contrasts strongly with the figure of De Klerk as man and architect, since he was sometimes depicted in somber tones. Enthusiastic, spontaneous, consciously melancholic, he was a scientist of the design as well as of the project, a master in the molding of materials, a virtuoso of the detail. De Klerk's imagery fed on his passion to fuse together science and art. Using again the language of *The Gay Science*, it is the "spiritual health" of the individual, who is capable of being a poet as well as a scientist, that allows him to practice a science in a manner not always *serious*.

Because of his search for a transfigured architecture, De Klerk could perhaps be associated with the magmatic events of German Expressionism, but his role was without a doubt unique. De Klerk represented the more concretely popular and accessible aspect of a cultural phenomenon that was obstinately intellectual. He was concerned with transforming a utopia of enigmatic symbols into a lexicon of solid forms with a precise meaning. At the same time, he was certainly able to project an architecture that broke away from historical continuity, in favor of a movement embracing the "new." In De Klerk's conception, the "new" was inseparable from the pursuit of complete freedom of expression, an idea also held by the German Expressionist

Michel de Klerk. Third block on the Spaarndammerplantsoen, Amsterdam, July 1917. Perspective of the inner court. Collection NDB, Amsterdam. Color page 21

artists and architects who, under the influence of Paul Scheerbart's pamphlet *Glasarchitektur,* saw the architecture of glass as a key to formulate a total utopia.[6] The strength of De Klerk's constructions had its origins in sentiments not dissimilar from the ones that gave birth to the Scheerbartian architecture: the meeting between man and nature, the transfiguration of common and public places.

De Klerk, however, never belonged to the *Gläserne Kette,* the "Glass Chain" that united the German Expressionist architects, and between the work of De Klerk and the *Glasarchitektur,* the *Alpine Architektur,* and the *Organische Architektur* of German Expressionism

there are rather substantial points of divergence. The same can be said of the different architectural results within the Amsterdam School. It is no accident that the Dutch school is characterized by the meeting of—if not by a true unity between—rigidity and expressionism; its slogans are the "certainty that knows" and the "power that can."

This positive desire, this tendency toward the composition and the physical construction rather than the ideological foundation, can be noticed in the work of Bruno Taut, who was strongly influenced by De Klerk's architecture. Attention has rarely been paid to the fact that Taut visited Holland just a few months after the more famous visit by

Erich Mendelsohn. Even Taut, who was one of the promoters of the Arbeitsrat für Kunst of Berlin and the architect to whom Scheerbart had dedicated his *Glasarchitektur,* expressed an opinion about Dutch architecture analogous to that of Mendelsohn. The latter, in a letter to his wife in which he analyzed the state of the new Dutch architecture, spoke of "visionary Amsterdam" and "analytical Rotterdam," predicting that national architecture could survive in the future only if the two tendencies were reconciled.[7]

Taut was convinced that Holland was at that time the most advanced country in the field of architecture. He visited Rotterdam and the minimal housing

Michel de Klerk. Competition design for a water tower in reinforced concrete, 1912. Watercolor and ink. Collection NDB, Amsterdam. Color page 28

project of Tusschendijken designed by J. J. P. Oud (1920–23) and noticed its extreme rationality. But he also studied the works of the Amsterdam School—the large housing blocks arranged with imagination and vivid with the colors of the various materials. While the rationalist Oud always criticized the Amsterdam group for their "lack of logic" and their "subjectivism," Taut instead found in their projects the confirmation of an old idea of his own: that architecture should go beyond merely the functional needs of construction to express something more. Like Mendelsohn, Taut recognized that the road to the future was the unification of the two schools.[8]

However, where Mendelsohn saw in the Amsterdam School an implicit parting from the path chosen by the Expressionists, Taut was greatly drawn toward the experiments of that group and of De Klerk in particular. He used such terms as "fantasy," "courage," and "comfort" when he referred to De Klerk, whom he defined as "a master gifted with great talent, who built the new residences according to the principles of a different architecture....his formal experiments, even those that seemed arbitrary, conferred on these first attempts a particular charm, and they stand out when compared with the products of the declining ordinary architecture."[9] Taut would demonstrate

this affinity in his own projects, especially in the houses at Schillerpark (Berlin-Wedding, 1924–25), where the expressive quality of the brick and the effect of plasticity recall the solutions adopted by De Klerk in the first block on the Spaarndammerplantsoen built for the housing association Eigen Haard.

The warm humanity of Taut, like that of De Klerk, was, however, far removed from the attitude of the functionalist Neues Bauen architects, who would consider "utopia as a technical neutrality."[10] Even so, the similarity between Taut and De Klerk should not encourage an immediate and superficial generalization. De Klerk's buildings are in fact very different from those of

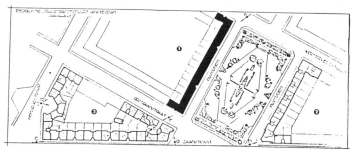

Michel de Klerk. First block on the Spaarndammerplantsoen, Amsterdam, 1913–14. Details: the cylinders

the German Expressionists, especially
when the latter gave a symbolic transfiguration to a purely functional detail.
De Klerk resisted any impulse to
manipulate the function. His imagination turned toward space, the perma-
nency of the materials, and the introduction of figures, which, with his
relish for the fragment, he disposed
liberally on the wall surfaces of his
architecture. In De Klerk's work, there
is no trace of that mysticism and sense
of unavoidable defeat that taints the
iconography of the Glass Architecture.
One senses, rather, a desire to create, to
"heighten the aspect of things to un-
precedented moments of joy, which in
their reality represent the most impor
tant elements of the joy of living."[11]

The experience of German Expressionism was marked by the tragic
events of the First World War, when it
seemed that a renewal could occur only
through the immolation of an entire
culture. This attitude was reflected in
Scheerbart's book *Lesabéndio*, in which
the artist-architect must fade out before
his astral planet is allowed to advance
toward its destiny. Faith in the future
depended on this sacrifice.[12] The Dutch,
however, were unfamiliar with this
nullifying will; they did not pose the
necessity of obliterating the past in
order to attain a cultural rebirth. De
Klerk, therefore, was not obliged to
reject angrily the previous culture. Instead, he renewed the traditional, using
whatever it had to offer that could be
useful to his aims. Lacking the intellectual and technological facility of
some of his contemporaries, he rejected
ideology in favor of the composition.

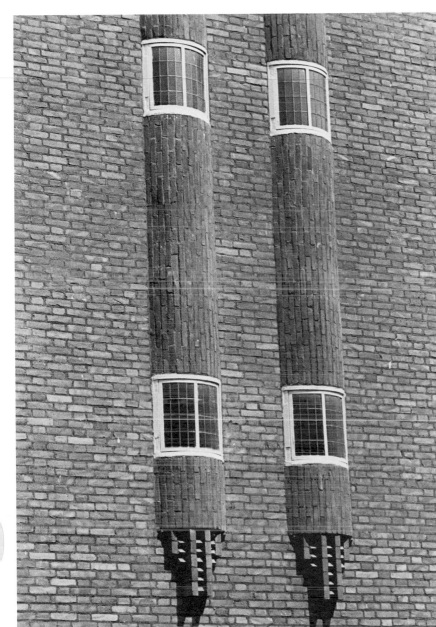

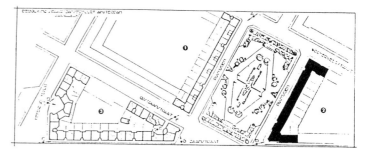

Michel de Klerk. Second block on the Spaarndammerplantsoen, Amsterdam, 1915-17. Color page 23. *Details: the textures*

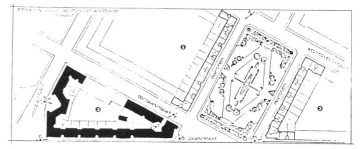

Michel de Klerk. Third block on the Spaarndammerplantsoen, Amsterdam, 1917–21.   Details: the windows

Scheerbart, in "Der Architekten-kongress," which appeared for the first time in *Frühlicht* in 1921, quotes the Italian architect Mirandulo: "We in Italy know very well what architecture is all about. Already in the last quarter of the century great numbers of architects came to admire our buildings done in brick. But today this no longer happens. Even the Italians know that architecture can develop now only by using iron, which makes any type of curve possible; and with reinforced cement we will be able to build a tower that leans even more than the Tower of Pisa."[13] De Klerk, on the other hand, never made use of the new technologies; instead, he preferred almost exclusively traditional methods of construction, which he consistently extended to the limit of their possibilities. More artisan than engineer, De Klerk always preferred brick to iron and multipane windows to solid sheets of glass. When building regulations forced him to break with conventional methods, De Klerk did it with a certain sense of embarrassment--in the tower of the third block on the Spaarndammerplantsoen, the internal structure in iron is completely hidden by a traditional covering of tiles. Thus, in examining the utopian effort of De Klerk, it is essential to recognize as its basis the absolute and undisputed importance of the construction and the supremacy of architecture over the laws governing the formation of the city.

This attitude is somewhat similar to what Manfredo Tafuri has called "the utopia of meaning" in his analysis of

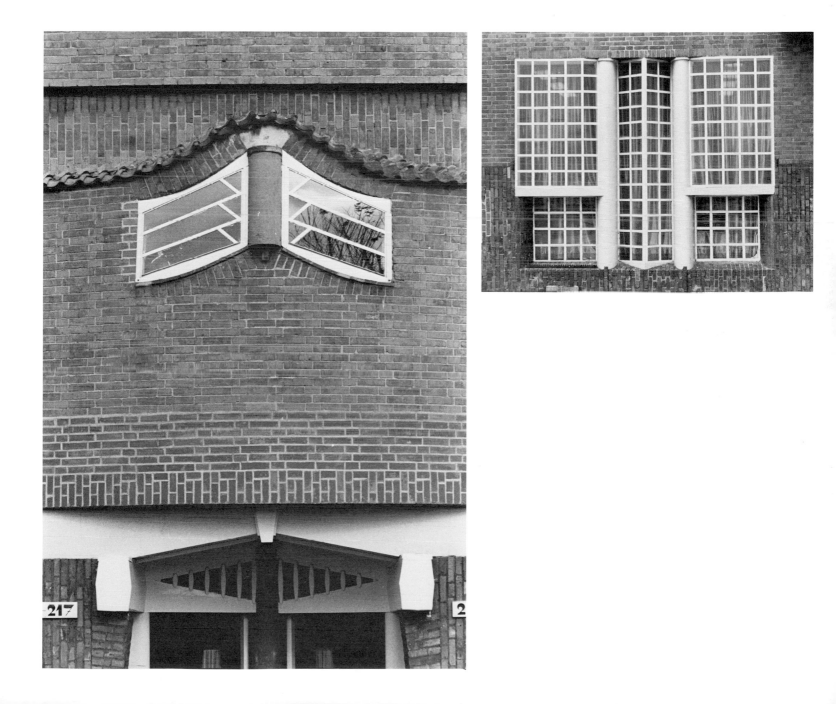

Michel de Klerk. Two sketches, house and tree, c. 1915. Pencil. Collection NDB, Amsterdam

the works of the German Expressionists Poelzig and Höger.[14] Like his German colleagues, De Klerk fought against the increasing tendency to abandon the image of the "ideal city." He charged his architecture with multiple symbols, signs, and suggestions capable of arresting this decline of identity. Once again, he acted in an original manner, exploiting the superimpositions and the vulgarizations introduced during the growth of the historical city, almost outlining in his buildings the complex events that had taken place in the course of history. If an event could not possibly have left a direct trace on a modern building, then De Klerk invented some imprints, even resorting to artifice. What are, in fact, all those details of unclear meaning that fill the architecture of the Spaarndammerplantsoen if not memories of an imagined past, the reuse, according to the medieval technique of recycling, of hypothetical fragments from ancestral forgotten buildings? They are there to prove the existence of the past and, therefore, the continuity of urban life. The way that De Klerk turned to the past and used freely and with an open mind whatever he found that could help his composition can be compared to the way that, in the Middle Ages, presumed relics of the heroic past of Christianity gave historical value to buildings.

This is the key to understanding De Klerk's architectural identity: the absolute belief in the expressive capacity of his buildings, born through a complete—almost obsessive—control of the

Michel de Klerk. Design for a postage stamp, c. 1915. Pencil and crayon. Collection NDB, Amsterdam

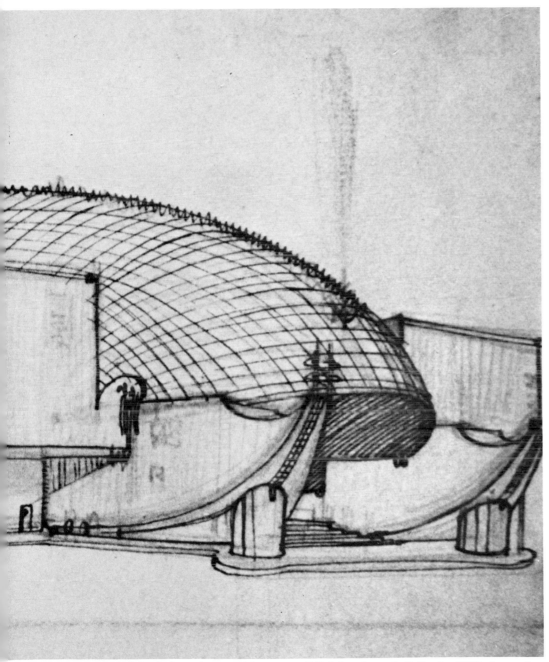

Michel de Klerk. Architectural fantasy, c. 1915. Ink and pencil. Collection NDB, Amsterdam

composition. It was noted that De Klerk was neither an orator nor a writer. He did not participate in public meetings, unless forced to. He spoke through his architecture, showing the commitment to concrete work that would characterize the following generations. His buildings are his moral acts. Through them one can perceive his determination to give a new meaning to urban growth.

After the lowering of its housing standards during the nineteenth century, Amsterdam found in De Klerk the perpetuator of its architectural tradition. This realized utopia arrested abruptly the recent history of poverty and degradation, and elevated the "worker's palace" to the status of priority in the construction of the city. De Klerk did this through the quality and intrinsic form of the architectural details and the unquestionable value of the composition.

With his architectural fantasies his "monuments"—De Klerk did not seem to try to propose, even allegorically, a social utopia. He limited himself to celebrating the work of man, emphasizing the role of the craftsman. In the preceding centuries, the same Dutch craftsmanship had found expression in shipbuilding. It is not accidental, perhaps, that the buildings at the Spaarndammerplantsoen are replete with references to the sea and the nautical world, and that its inhabitants conferred on the third block the nickname "Het Schip" (The Ship) because of its form.

This reference to the sea leads to one

Michel de Klerk. Two designs for a two-family house in Amsterdam, c. 1915.
From Wendingen *6, nos. 4–5 (1924), p. 17*

last parallel, which may provide more insight into De Klerk's work. Le Corbusier wrote:

> If we forget for a moment that a steamship is a machine for transport and look at it with a fresh eye, we shall feel that we are facing an important manifestation of temerity, of discipline, of harmony, of a beauty that is calm, vital and strong.
>
> A seriously-minded architect, looking at it as an architect (i.e. a creator of organisms), will find in a steamship his freedom from an age-long but contemptible enslavement to the past.[15]

This was written in 1923. It is important to note that De Klerk at that time also showed a strong sensitivity for naval construction. However, to Le Corbusier's transatlantic ships and the systematic technology in the building of great passenger liners, De Klerk opposed the image of the nautical tradition of his own country, of its wooden ships and of the busy trading of Holland's golden age.

Indeed, he gave the motto *Gouden Eeuw* (Golden Age) to a poster he designed for a competition in 1912 that was to publicize a great national exhibition of shipbuilding. In his sketch, he depicted a galleon of baroque proportions, triumphantly sailing into the open sea.[16] Certainly the reference could not have been different in a city like Amsterdam, which lived under the shadow of the *koggeschip*, a fast-sailing mercantile ship of the Middle Ages. The

image of this big-bellied flat ship, which had brought prosperity to the city, can be seen on the highest spire of the old town hall (now the Royal Palace), as well as on the ancient seals of the city. Thus, it was not the spirit of the sleek ocean liner *Aquitania* that stirred De Klerk's imagination,[17] but rather the spirit of the admiral ships of the Dutch fleet in the 1600s, or of the ships belonging to the East India Company, or, more simply, of the boats of the Zuiderzee with their movable keels and complex carpentry.

Continuing with this bold nautical analogy, Le Corbusier affirmed that "the steamship is the first stage in the realization of a world organized according to the new spirit."[18] But, here again, De Klerk saw in the metaphor of shipbuilding a way of renewing the trea-

sures of the past rather than a guide to a utopian future. He was attracted to the formal richness of its craftsmanship, showing a marked preference for the shipyard carpenter over the naval engineer. Nevertheless, one can see in this also a kind of social utopia. A legion of patient and useful workers found in De Klerk a courageous pioneer in the battle for the superfluous, for things not strictly utilitarian, for the abhorred "luxury." We should not smile at this, because, when De Klerk's plans for the Spaarndammerplantsoen were submitted to the City Council and the Schoonheidscommissie of Amsterdam, it was exactly this aspect that—even before discussing costs—drew censure from some of the members. The same criticism was later repeated by the defenders of ascetic rationalism. About these, Banham

Michel de Klerk. Third block on the Spaarndammerplantsoen, "Het Schip" (The Ship), Amsterdam, c. 1923. Photograph, Collection Gemeentelijke Dienst Volkshuisvesting, Amsterdam

wrote, "one of the aspects of his work, as in the Spaarndam housing, that has given offence to Rationalists ever since it was built, is the air of mild luxury it exudes, a luxury felt to be somehow improper to mass-housing."[19]

On behalf of the urban working class, De Klerk fought for freedom from the obligation of using only the essential. In this fight, he used the rediscovery of the craftsmanship that had formed the basis of the triumphs of Dutch naval carpentry. He applied those same techniques to housing. This is proved by the many symbols that punctuate the buildings, symbols drawn from that abundance of images that constitute the collective heritage of an unforgotten past. It is the collective heritage of a nation and the continuous joy of illusion; the interplay between presence and absence, the ethereal expression of a dreamed world. Michelangelo, then, perhaps was right when he reportedly sharply criticized the Dutch people for their tendency to daydream. He said:

> In the Netherlands they paint mainly to reproduce the exterior appearance of things, preferably subjects that provoke enthusiasm or are irreproachable, like saints or prophets. In most cases, they paint what is usually called a landscape, but they fill it with figures....It is an attempt to reproduce simultaneously, and with great perfection, many disparate things, while only one of them would require the dedication of all the energies.[20]

Michel de Klerk. Competition design for the poster of the "Eerste Nederlandsche Tentoonstelling op Scheepvaartgebied" (First Dutch Nautical Exposition) in Amsterdam, motto Gouden Eeuw *(Golden Age), 1912. Collection NDB, Amsterdam.* Below: *Preparatory sketch;* opposite: *final design*

NOTES

1. For the relationship between De Klerk and the German Expressionists see Reyner Banham, *Theory and Design in the First Machine Age* (London and New York, 1960), pp. 163–84; Dennis Sharp, *Modern Architecture and Expressionism* (New York, 1966), pp. 131–43; Wolfgang Pehnt, *Expressionist Architecture* (London, 1973), pp. 181–93; Manfredo Tafuri and Francesco Dal Co, *Architettura Contemporanea* (Milan, 1976), pp. 162–65.

2. The definition was coined by De Klerk himself in a note written for the sixtieth birthday of H. P. Berlage, in *Bouwkundig Weekblad* 36, no. 45 (1916), p. 332.

3. G. Colli, Introductory Note to F. Nietzsche, *La Gaia Scienza* (Milan, 1979), p. 7.

4. The references to Nietzsche's thought are taken from the analysis developed by M. Cacciari, "Sulla Genesi del Pensiero Negativo," *Contropiano,* no. 1 (1969) and by Manfredo Tafuri, *Progetto e Utopia* (Bari, 1973).

5. Piet Kramer, "De bouwwerken van M. de Klerk," *Wendingen,* nos. 9–10 (1924), p. 3. Cited in Wolfgang Pehnt, op. cit. (note 1), p. 190.

6. Paul Scheerbart, *Glasarchitektur* (Berlin, 1914). This book, which Scheerbart dedicated to Bruno Taut, is a dream treated in the form of a brief architectural treatise; it is assumed that the transition to a new era of glass occurred as a result of a heroic encounter between nature and technique. See Reyner Banham, "The Glass Paradise," *The Architectural Review* 125, no. 745 (1959), pp. 87–89; Dennis Sharp, ed., *Glass Architecture by Paul Scheerbart and Alpine Architecture by Bruno Taut* (New York and Washington, D.C., 1972); Giuseppe Samonà, "Saggio Introduttivo" to *Frühlicht. Gli anni dell'avanguardia architettonica in Germania* (Milan, 1974); Rosemarie Haag Bletter, "Paul Scheerbart's Architectural Fantasies," *Journal of the Society of Architectural Historians* 34, no. 2 (May 1975), pp. 83–97.

   On the subject of the Arbeitsrat für Kunst and of the *Gläserne Kette,* see Marcel S. Franciscono, *Walter Gropius and the Creation of the Bauhaus in Weimar: The Ideals and Artistic Theories of Its Founding Years* (Chicago: University of Illinois Press, 1971), Rosemarie Haag Bletter, "The Interpretation of the Glass Dream—Expressionist Architecture and the History of the Crystal Metaphor," *Journal of the Society of Architectural Historians* 40, no. 1 (1981), pp. 20–43.

7. O. Beyer, ed., *Erich Mendelsohn, Letters of an Architect* (London, 1967), pp. 59–60.

8. K. Junghanns, *Bruno Taut 1880–1938* (Milan, 1978), pp. 34–35. For literature about Taut, see Rosemarie Haag Bletter, "Bruno Taut and Paul Scheerbart's Vision: Utopian Aspects of German Expressionist Architecture," Ph.D. dissertation, Columbia University, 1973–74.

9. Bruno Taut, *Die Neue Baukunst in Europa und in Amerika* (Stuttgart, 1929), p. 41.

10. Manfredo Tafuri and Francesco Dal Co, op. cit. (note 1), p. 168.

11. Piet Kramer, Note in memoriam of M. de Klerk, *Architectura* 28, no. 38 (1923), p. 240.

12. Paul Scheerbart, *Lesabèndio. Ein Asteröiden-Roman* (Munich and Leipzig, 1913). Scheerbart's text describes the existence of the inhabitants of the asteroid Pallas, whose purpose in life is to make "their planet more resplendent." Lesabèndio, one of the community's leaders, agrees to dissolve himself into the body of a planet in order to form, together with other brother planets, a radiant crown around the sun.

13. Paul Scheerbart, "Der Architektenkongress," *Frühlicht* 1 (Autumn 1921).

14. Manfredo Tafuri and Francesco Dal Co, op. cit. (note 1), p. 162.

15. Le Corbusier, *Towards a New Architecture* (London, 1946), pp. 96–97.

16. The "Eerste Nederlandsche Tentoonstelling op Scheepvaartgebied" (First Dutch Nautical Exposition) was held in Amsterdam between June and September 1913. A competition for the design of the exhibition's poster was held a year earlier. Of the ninety-nine entries submitted, only four reached the stage of final selection. Among these was no. 28, *Gouden Eeuw* (Golden Age) by De Klerk, which the jury found of a "festive character, truly the celebration of an event." Nevertheless, C. Rol's design was awarded first prize.

17. In the chapter dedicated to the "Paquebots" of his book *Towards a New Architecture*, Le Corbusier presents as meaningful examples of the "new spirit" a few modern trans-atlantic liners, among them the *Aquitania* of the Cunard Line. Le Corbusier, op. cit. (note 15), pp. 81–97.

18. Le Corbusier, op. cit. (note 15), p. 97.

19. Reyner Banham, op. cit. (note 1), p. 165.

20. J. Huizinga, *L'Autunno del Medioevo* (Florence, 1953), p. 379. This book, *Herfsttij der Middeleeuwen*, was first published in Holland in 1919. The earliest English edition, *The Waning Middle Ages*, appeared in 1924, published in London.

Petra Timmer

THE AMSTERDAM SCHOOL AND INTERIOR DESIGN: ARCHITECTS AND CRAFTSMEN AGAINST THE RATIONALISTS

THE Amsterdam School was not alone in envisaging a revolution in the design of furniture and interiors no less than of buildings. Several other architectural movements born during the first quarter of the century shared the idea that the building must be a *Gesamtkunstwerk*, a totality. Prominent among these groups were the rationalists, who dominated Dutch architecture until the end of the First World War. Despite this fundamental point of agreement, the Amsterdam School architects differed from the rationalists in their belief that the interior derived from and was subservient to the exterior, and they scorned the products of the rationalists as being unimaginative and austere.

The genesis of the Amsterdam School's conception of interior design— or "spatial design," as it was sometimes called—can be traced in the pages of *Wendingen*, the monthly publication that was the mouthpiece of the group. In the very first issue, of January 1918, editor-in-chief H. Th. Wijdeveld rhapsodized about "unbridled fantasies in free flight…unto the coasts of Utopia."[1] His words evoke the expressionist bent of the Amsterdam School, which subordinated logical organization to emotional resonance, and the revelation of structure to suggestive ornamental detail. Not surprisingly, several authors in the first issue of *Wendingen* attacked the rationalists for failing to satisfy the human need for warmth and comfort. They were accused of imposing rules that were overly rigid and, in any case,

J. Gidding. Rugs and decorative painting, entrance of Tuschinski Theater, 1920–21. Photograph, Collection Historisch Topographische Atlas, Gemeentelijke Archiefdienst, Amsterdam

unnecessary for the construction of good furniture.[2]

One of the contributors exulted that:

> fortunately, there has arisen a new generation that has an eye for form and color, and considers no single material inferior for its purposes. Purified by a correct insight into rationalism, [this group] is trying to recapture lost ground.[3]

He was referring to the Amsterdam School, which opposed rigorous theorizing, preferring to rely on the individual's intuition.[4] Although each member would develop his own formal idiom, most work associated with the group, particularly during the "classic years" of 1918–23, was characterized by a strong plasticity.

Those who moved in the *Wendingen* orbit agreed that all the parts of a building, whether two-dimensional (for example, wallpaper and carpets) or three-dimensional (furniture, sculptural details), should be based on the same design concept, so that the entire interior environment would be consistent with the architectural whole. However, whether the architect alone should design everything—the building, its interiors and their contents—or should employ the services of a decorative artist was a disputed issue, even among those who pursued the same formal goals.

Two strong advocates of autonomy for the decorative designer[5] came to the fore during the period when the Amsterdam School was formulating its ideals of free plastic expression. One was W. Penaat (1875–1957), who held a central position within the Vereeniging voor Ambachts-en Nijverheids Kunst (VANK: Association for Crafts and Industrial Arts), which had been founded in 1904 to promote the interests of the applied arts and therefore also to challenge architectural domination of interior design.[6] In 1914 Penaat, with the architect Jan Gratama, planned a Nederlandse Driebond (Dutch Triple Federation) that would bring together industry, commerce, and art to achieve better quality in the design of Dutch products. This organization was inspired by the successful Deutsche Werkbund, founded in 1907.[7] At this time there was current in socialist-oriented circles the utopian idea that everyone should live in a beautiful environment, which would lead to happiness and justice. Replacing the "junk and trash" in the home of the working man by beautifully designed everyday objects would make him a more fulfilled human being.[8]

The outbreak of the First World War prevented the implementation of the Driebond idea, but in 1917 Penaat again advanced his plan. He presented his views in the journal *Architectura*, published by Architectura et Amicitia,[9] the same organization that would sponsor *Wendingen*. Indeed, the entire issue of *Architectura* devoted to the Driebond

Piet Kramer. Interior of De Bijenkorf, The Hague, 1926. From De Bijenkorf 's Gravenhage (Amsterdam, 1926)

proposal, which was designed by Wijde-veld, may be considered an experimental forerunner of *Wendingen*.[10] However, several contributors to the Drie-bond issue did not agree with Penaat's proposal to cooperate with industry, for they feared that mechanical production would fetter the artistic freedom necessary to achieve beauty. Nevertheless, Penaat's initiative laid the basis for the increased independence and the improved status of the decorative artist.

The other significant figure in the development of the interior design profession played his role within the ranks of *Wendingen*. This was the architect J. L. M. Lauweriks, who, with K. P. C. de Bazel, had founded one of the first ateliers, in 1895, for decorative arts in the Netherlands.[11] During a portion of his thirteen-year stay in Germany, from 1904 to 1917, Lauweriks had served as director of the Handfertigkeits Seminar, a crafts school in Hagen. A theosophist with an esoteric and mystical view of life, Lauweriks had been greatly taken with the Expressionism that was being manifested in German pictorial art at the time.[12] Upon his return to Amsterdam in 1917, Lauweriks became head of the Quellinus School, an influential teaching institution for the arts and crafts that had been founded in 1879.

Lauweriks's aim was to give the interior decorator his own identity and to liberate him from subordination to the architect. To this end, he separated instruction in furniture design from architectural training, eliminating in the process the school's department of architectural drafting. At the same time, he modified the nature of instruction given at the school, emphasizing practice over theory. Like others in the *Wendingen* circle, Lauweriks was suspicious of theory. He believed design was mainly a question of feeling and unhampered creativity, which one could not learn from books.

In his own work, he focused attention on the surfaces of objects and on the materials employed. His designs for interiors feature brilliantly hued patterns that animate the two-dimensional wall planes, and the exteriors of such buildings as the J. Thorn Prikker house in Hagen of 1910 display textural and tonal contrasts of wood, brick, and stone. In his work as well as through his teaching, therefore, he greatly influenced the coloristic and tactile aspects of design among members of the Amsterdam School.[13]

Through his position at the prestigious Quellinus School, Lauweriks was able to legitimize expressive decorative design in the Netherlands. Although contrasting views existed about the proper role of the interior designer— some of *Wendingen*'s editors tended to dismiss "furniture makers who call themselves architects,"[14]—the ideal of the "expressive total work of architecture" among both architects and designers emerged triumphant after the end of the First World War.

Thus Wijdeveld's reaction to work done at the Quellinus School under the direction of Lauweriks was positive— and characteristically overwrought:

Like a lightning bolt, a fiercely burning celestial torch glitters through the students' ornamental designs, symbolic of the inexorable will [of Lauweriks] that dominates the school. In all the projects, the play of lines achieves an unrivaled whimsicality, the gamut of colors results in unorthodox combinations, the form-giving attains an irregular harmony. Axial symmetry, so long considered the only basis of design, is avoided, yet here and there can still be discerned a geometric figure, present as if by accident. Everywhere free motifs appear to grow, rootless, from the field of ornamentation. The decorative element reigns supreme, in feverish reaction against the excessive rationality imposed by the [main] architectonic directions of the last twenty years.[15]

It was at this juncture of two- and three-dimensional design that the concept of the expressive totality was perfected. Far more possibilities were opened through the fusing of exterior and interior than were available with the rationalist approach to design. Just as a building's skin could be given decorative emphasis through the color and shape of the bricks and the addition of sculpture, wrought iron, and stained glass to the surfaces, so too could ornamentation be applied to furniture, through textiles, veneers of different kinds of wood, and so on.

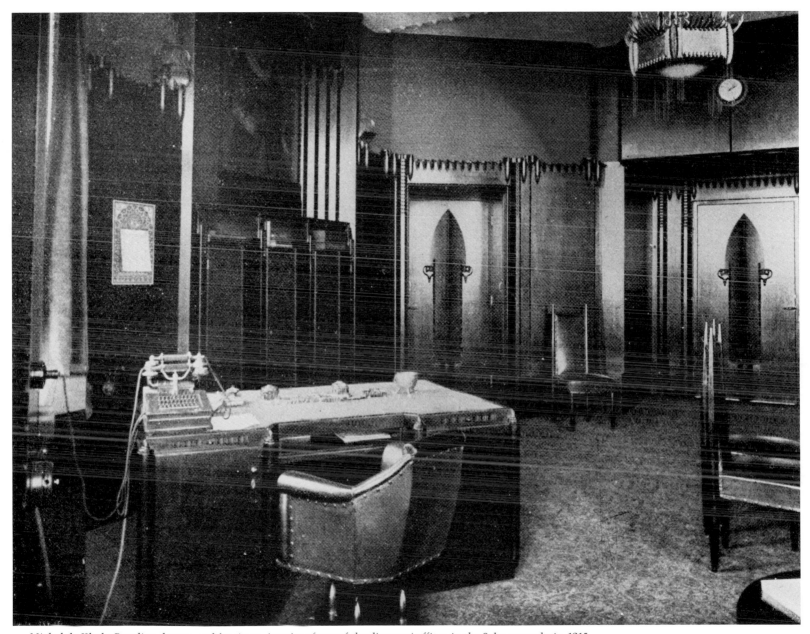

Michel de Klerk. Paneling, lamps, and furniture, interior of one of the directors' offices in the Scheepvaarthuis, 1915. From S. G. Hirsch, Het Scheepvaarthuis, n.d.

One way of achieving expressive totality was by repeating the same motif—as mirror images or enlargements or reductions of the same form—in rugs and tapestries, stained glass, wallpaper, and curtains. Through the interaction of pattern and color an imaginative, enchanting atmosphere could be created. Particularly fine examples of such a total concept include the Scheepvaarthuis (Shipping Building, 1912–16) and the Tuschinski Theater (1918–21), both in Amsterdam, and the Hague branch (1926) of the department store De Bijenkorf (The Beehive), designed by Piet Kramer. De Bijenkorf's impact was lyrically described in an advertising text by P. H. Ritter:

> Instead of trying to disguise the prosaic nature of a commercial space by means of fake Ionic columns, we find in De Bijenkorf a department store transformed into a fairytale palace. I can imagine no more captivating series of tales than those of Scheherazade, which are recalled as one wanders through De Bijenkorf.[16]

In the home no less than in such public structures, the same effects of a magical atmosphere were sought. Almost all publications of the teens and twenties concerned with interiors, even those not representing the expressionist direction, praised consistency, intimacy, quiet, and harmony.[17] These qualities could be achieved through the

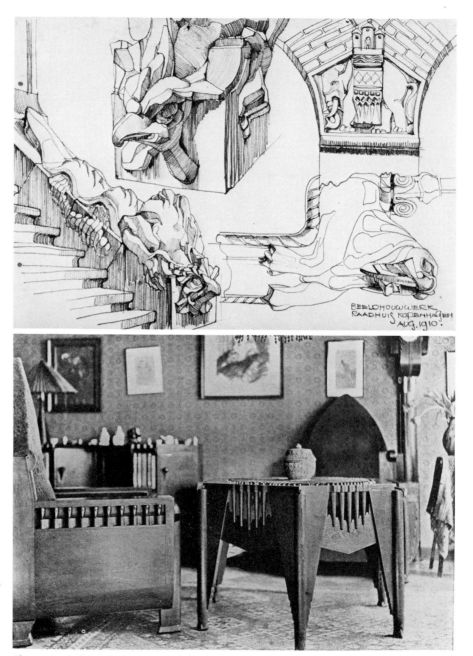

Above: *Michel de Klerk. Studies of the sculpture on Copenhagen's town hall, 1920. Pencil. Collection NDB, Amsterdam*
Below: *Michel de Klerk. Furniture, interior of Dr. J. Polenaar, Amsterdam, 1913. From* Wendingen 7, No. 10 (1925–26), p. 14

Michel de Klerk. Furniture, model dining room in 't Woonhuys, 1916. From Wendingen 7, *no. 10 (1925–26), p. 10*

judicious coordinating of the shapes and colors of household furnishings, and through the proper proportioning of the length, height, and width of the room. When, as in older houses, ceiling and window heights were excessive, and too much light was admitted, remedial steps could be taken. It was recommended, for example, that walls be sectioned horizontally, by means of wallpaper or paneling, using dark colors for the bottom portion to create the illusion of a lower space. The glaring light from tall windows could be mitigated by covering the upper part with curtains or by installing stained glass.[18] To suggest strength and sturdiness, the floor area should be dark in color. Through these means was obtained "that play of light in which furniture and other household objects could lead their quiet and meditative lives."[19]

Admittedly, it was somewhat difficult to realize the total concept in the home, for rarely was an artist commissioned to design a private house in its entirety or to essay a major remodeling of a rented dwelling. Nevertheless, several members of the Amsterdam School succeeded in making a mark on domestic interior design, the most distinguished being Piet Kramer, Hildo Krop, and Michel de Klerk. Of these, De Klerk offers the broadest scope for study, since few of Kramer's furniture projects have survived, while Krop, municipal sculptor of Amsterdam from 1916 on, was only incidentally occupied with furnishings, although his designs from 1915 to 1917 are considered fun-

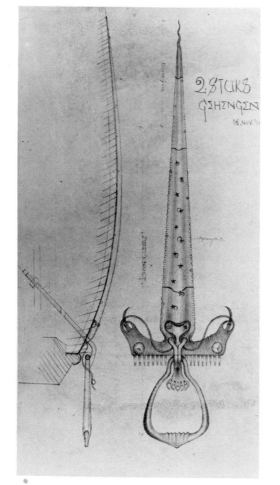

damental to the emerging artistry of the Amsterdam School. Happily, there exists a fairly complete archive for De Klerk, at once the most inspiring and enigmatic of the trio.[20]

From 1905 on there are autograph interior designs by De Klerk (see pages 68, 69), and from 1913 to 1920 he executed a number of pieces of furniture. Predictably, his earliest work continues the style devised by his mentor, Eduard Cuypers, and is linearly ornamented. While working for Cuypers, De Klerk was exposed to furniture that incorporated elements of English and German fin-de-siècle motifs, but at the same time he was introduced to European folk art. When in 1910 he traveled to Denmark and Sweden, he made not only travel sketches but also drawings of heavily decorated peasant furniture. The sculptures of monsters and awesome animal heads on the facade of Copenhagen's town hall of 1892–1905 by Martin Nyrop (1849–1921) seem to have impressed him as well.[21]

Parabolic motifs, both truncated and complete, first appear in the pieces De Klerk designed in 1913 for Dr. J. Polenaar, which are still relatively sober. His architectural designs for that year show the same novel shapes, which he would subsequently employ often, together with the trapezoid. Then De Klerk's furniture became more plastic, as can be seen in the objects he made in 1915 for the Scheepvaarthuis. The contours have become rounder and the decoration richer and more fantastic. This is particularly apparent in the furniture he designed for the firm 't Woonhuys (The

Dwelling) during 1916 and 1917. Here are found sculptural motifs that evoke strong associations of the animal world. Particularly aggressive crustaceans like crabs and lobsters seem to have settled upon or within these pieces, making the user the apparent target of vicious claws and teeth.[22] Other striking shapes, reminiscent of the fabled Middle Eastern atmosphere of the *Thousand and One Nights*, seem related to Aladdin's breeches and pointed shoes.[23] Sled-shaped feet under chairs and armchairs, which occur frequently, create an impression of mobility—unjustified, since the furniture is as heavy as lead.

De Klerk, with his often incomprehensible details, succeeded in evoking a mysterious atmosphere, but some also found it unsettling, if not hostile. Thus Wijdeveld, while describing De Klerk's furniture as fantastic, whimsical, and spontaneous, remarked that the pieces were evidence of a depressive, albeit searching, mind: "prophets of doom, like music in a minor key."[24]

Less baffling are the designs by Kramer, who, like De Klerk, was also an architect. These contain fewer flourishes, and the decoration is less exuberant. The designer W. Retera called Kramer's furniture "sensuously succulent," and observed that the pieces "seem to express in a single sentence what is in the heart."[25]

Kramer's furniture, and also that by Krop, is more robust, tactile, and compact than De Klerk's. The tactile aspect of Krop's work is particularly noteworthy. Krop regularly applied minutely carved wooden details to the surface

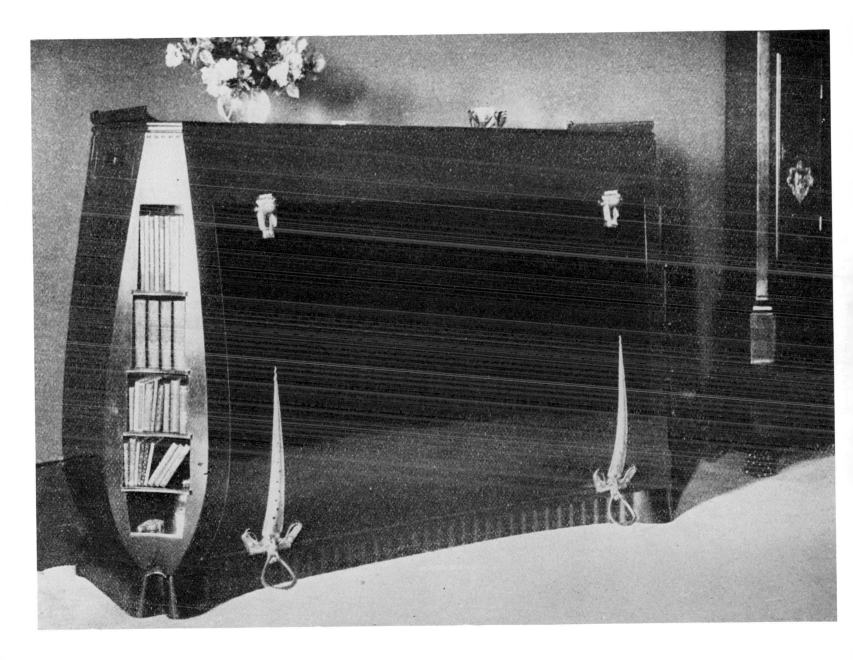

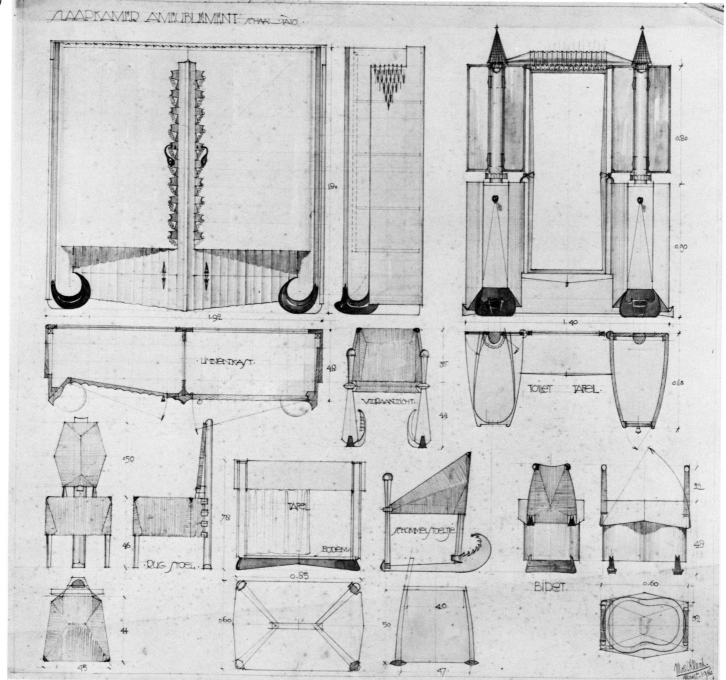

Opposite: *Michel de Klerk. Design for a bedroom suite for 't Woonhuys, 1916. Collection NDB, Amsterdam*

Michel de Klerk. Armchair, c. 1916. Photograph, Collection NDB, Amsterdam

Michel de Klerk. Design for a mantelpiece, 1919. Collection NDB, Amsterdam

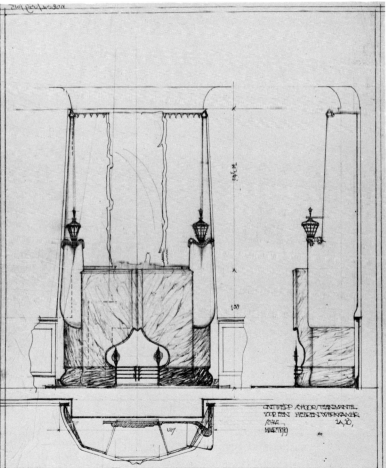

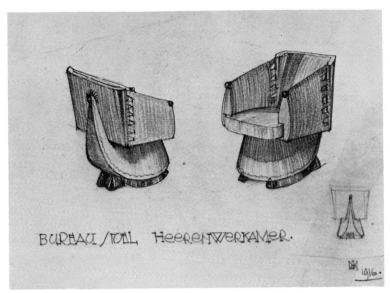

BUREAU /TOEL HEERENWERKAMER.

Opposite: *Michel de Klerk. Interior for 't Woonhuys, 1916. From* Wendingen 7, *no. 10 (1925–26), p. 9. This suite was also shown at the Paris World's Fair in 1925*

Left. *Michel de Klerk. Design for a desk chair for a "gentleman's study," 1916. Collection NDB, Amsterdam*

Below: *Michel de Klerk. Design for the living room of Huize Overbosch, Crailo, 1920. Collection NDB, Amsterdam*

of his furniture, reflecting his background as a sculptor.

Regarding the question of mass production of furniture, the three men were ambivalent. De Klerk, for example, was in principle strongly opposed to the idea. In the Driebond issue he wrote:

> A piece of furniture, with its small scale, refined luster and supple plasticity, is entirely different in essence from a utensil, which has as little to do with the concept of construction as, for example, cattle raising. [Furniture design] require[s] continual study and attention. In my case it was a matter of reproducing a single type but six or seven times, but in actual mass production there could be no question of such integrity in terms of interior art.[26]

Nevertheless, De Klerk had greater freedom when reproducing a few objects in series for a firm like 't Woonhuys than when designing for an individual client. Kramer and Krop also worked for furniture stores during the war, the former at Nusink and Son in Amsterdam, the latter at Mutters in The Hague. Although Krop was considered the most socially motivated of the three, it is not known whether he designed furniture for mass production. Kramer designed the interior of a worker's dwelling for the "Amsterdam Interior Design Exhibition" held at the Stedelijk Museum in 1921. It was hoped

Opposite: *Ch. Bartels. Ladies' parlor, 1918. From VANK-jaarboek 1920, fig. 16*

H. Krop. Furniture suite for Mr. and Mrs. Polak-Krop, Steenwijk, 1915. Executed by H. P. Mutters and Son, The Hague. Photograph, Collection Gemeentemuseum, The Hague

Opposite: *Piet Kramer. Parlor suite for Dr. G., Amsterdam, 1920. Furniture executed by NV v/h Randoe, Haarlem, 1921. Photograph, Collection NDB, Amsterdam*

Left: *J. Boterenbrood. Tea table. Collection Stedelijk Museum, Amsterdam*

Below: *D. Greiner. Design for an easy chair, 1922–23. Collection NDB, Amsterdam*

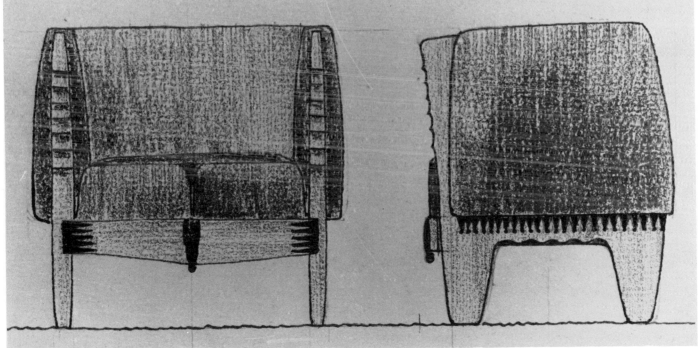

that such displays would influence industry to manufacture well-designed objects, thereby making good and affordable products available to the working class.[27]

Architects were willing to concern themselves with furniture in this period because of the war. The supply of raw materials was insufficient for the construction of dwellings, but there was enough wood to make furniture. Moreover, because of war profiteering, there was much money (often "black" or illegal) in circulation that could be lavished on luxury objects. So the Amsterdam School designers, perhaps from pragmatic more than idealistic considerations, switched to commercial furniture design during the war. However, a profitable future was envisioned for architecture as a whole and the accompanying arts and crafts for the period after the war, when raw materials would again be more readily available.[28]

Certainly in the area of two-dimensional decorative design, there was a great flowering immediately after the war. Designers freed themselves from too much reliance on a geometric system and indulged their imaginations.[29] In this, the Quellinus School had led the way.

One of the most popular mediums was stained glass, which had come into favor because of its modulating effect and its qualities that contributed to the longed-for "expressive spaciousness." Stained glass is in fact a complex medium, two- and three-dimensional at the same time, promoting separation as well as translucent permeation. Stained-glass designers worked in a variety of styles, and were active in both commercial production and the creation of unique pieces. The well-known artist W. Bogtman, who had a large studio in Haarlem (still in existence today), executed the stained glass for the Scheepvaarthuis, among other projects. Designers in this field also worked for 't Woonhuys.

Wrought iron was similarly ambiguous, being simultaneously open and enclosing. Because it was rather expensive, it was employed less frequently, but was used three-dimensionally in such objects as lamps, clocks, and fireplaces.

Initially, wallpaper had to be imported from abroad, and came chiefly from Germany. Only in 1917 was wallpaper designed in the Netherlands, by L. Zwiers, for the lithographic firm Dieperink and Co. in Amsterdam. Subsequently, other wallpaper factories were founded, and they commissioned artists to design patterns. However, the Amsterdam School ideal of expressive spaciousness was somewhat elusive as far as wallpaper is concerned because of the flatness of the surface to which it is attached. The same is true, though to a lesser degree, of home textiles, rugs, and tapestries. By means of their pleats, curtains could gain a certain bulkiness, and fabrics with a special texture or nap could also create a three-dimensional effect. Rugs and tablecloths could enhance the plasticity of floors and tables through their patterns.

Thus the concept of the total en-

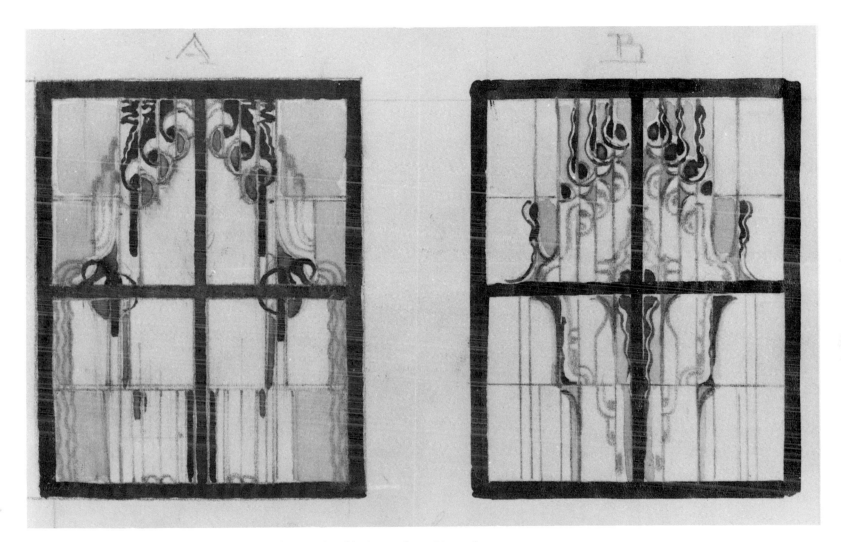

W. Bogtman. Design for stained-glass windows commissioned by 't Woonhuys. Watercolor.
Collection NDB, Amsterdam

Opposite: *L. Zwiers. Lithographed wallpaper, 1920. From C. J. A. Begeer*, Holland, Sier-en Nijverheids kunst *(n.p., 1927)*

J. Gidding. Smyrna rug, 1920. From VANK-jaarboek 1921, fig. 67

vironment, even if seldom completely realized, reigned for at least a decade as a guiding ideal among all those associated with the Amsterdam School, whether architect or designer. But, after 1923, various factors brought about a change in the attitude toward two- and three-dimensional design. De Klerk's death in that year led to a certain slackening in the drive of the Amsterdam School, and the exuberant individualism that had marked its productions was tempered. Rich details were pruned and the full contours of the furniture were slimmed down as curves gave way to straighter lines. The reaction against expressive freedom in design favored functionalism and factory production, a development that was fostered by a gradually deepening economic crisis, which prescribed greater sobriety. Penaat's Driebond idea now found support; in 1923 De Bond voor Kunst in Industrie (BKI: The Federation for Arts in Industry) was founded by manufacturers to promote the better design of Dutch industrial products.

By 1930, those who favored a cool, rational functionalism gained the upper hand. In contrast to the artists of the Amsterdam School, these designers had as their goal repetitive, open, and simply furnished interiors. In their pursuit of economically produced surroundings for the common man, they laid a taboo on luxury. The whimsical fantasies and the dark, intimate environments of the Amsterdam School came to an end, leaving in their wake the memory of a beautiful and mysterious dream world.

NOTES

This article is based primarily on the following works: Frans van Burkom, "Kunstvormgeving in Nederland," in *Nederlandse architectuur 1910–1930, Amsterdamse School* (Amsterdam: Stedelijk Museum, 1975), pp. 71–108; Frans van Burkom, "L'Arte degli interni e del Mobile," in Giovanni Fanelli and Ezio Godoli, eds., *Wendingen 1918–1931, Documenti dell' arte olandese del Novecento* (Florence: Centro Di, 1982), pp. 57–64; Frans van Burkom and Wim de Wit, "Vormgeving als kunst, kunst als Vormgeving," in *Nederlandse architectuur 1910–1930*, op. cit., pp. 34–40.

I am particularly grateful for Helen Searing's gracious and intelligent assistance in preparing this article.

Opposite: *Michel de Klerk. Wrought-iron lamp in one of the directors' offices of the Scheepvaart-huis, 1915. Executed by H. J. Winkelman*

H. Krop. Cast-bronze pendulum clock. Collection Stedelijk Museum, Amsterdam

1. H. Th. Wijdeveld, "Wendingen," *Wendingen* 1, no. 1 (1918), p. 1.

2. P. H. Endt, "Over rationalisme in de meubelkunst," *Wendingen* 1, no. 3 (1918), pp. 15–16.

3. M. J. Granpré Molière, "De tweespalt in de hedendaagsche kunst," *Wendingen* 1, no. 4 (1918), pp. 6–10.

4. See Piet Kramer, "Verandering," *Wendingen* 1, no. 7 (1918), pp. 11–12.

5. "Interior architecture" became an autonomous profession only much later. Cf. P. Fuhring and R. Eggink, "De binnenhuis-architekt: profilering van een beroep," *Binnenhuis architektuur in Nederland 1900–1981* (The Hague, 1981), pp. 38–47.

6. During the twenties and thirties, VANK greatly stimulated appreciation for the applied arts through several publications, the VANK yearbooks *(VANK-jaarboeken)* and the series *De Toegepaste Kunsten in Nederland*, which reviewed crafts as well as factory-produced objects for daily use.

7. For the Deutsche Werkbund, see *Zwischen Kunst und Industrie: Der Deutsche Werkbund* (Munich: Staatliches Museum für Angewandte Kunst, 1975) and Lucius Burckhardt, ed., *The Werkbund: History and Ideology 1907–1933* (New York: Barron's, 1980).

8. *Jac. van den Bosch en de vernieuwing van het Binnenhuis*, exhibition catalogue (Haarlem: Frans Halsmuseum: 1976), p. 3.

9. Architectura et Amicitia was founded in 1855. This architectural society published a

number of periodicals, including *Architectura* (1893–1917; 1921–26) and *Wendingen* (1918–31).

10. The Driebond issue appeared as a special issue in *Architectura* 25, nos. 39–40 (1917). This issue was also published separately, with separate paging.

11. Nic. H. M. Tummers, *J. L. Mathieu Lauweriks, Zijn werk en zijn invloed op architectuur en vormgeving rond 1910: "De Hagener impuls"* (Hilversum, 1968).

12. Cf. J. L. M. Lauweriks, "Het decoratieve en het constructieve," *VANK-jaarboek*, 1920, pp. 7–14.

13. For more information about Lauweriks's educative method, see M. Trappeniers, "Mathieu Lauweriks als leraar in het kunstnijverheidsonderwijs," *Nederlands Kunsthistorisch Jaarboek* 1979, v. 30 (Haarlem, 1980), pp. 173–96.

14. J. L. M. Lauweriks, "Indrukken ener Tentoonstelling," *Wendingen* 1, no. 6 (1918), p. 327.

15. H. Th. Wijdeveld, "Kunstnijverheidsschool Quellinus. Tentoonstelling van werk der leerlingen," *Wendingen* 1, no. 7 (1918), pp. 12–15.

16. Dr. P. H. Ritter, Jr., "Het Paleis der Levensvreugde," in *De Bijenkorf, 's Gravenhage* (Amsterdam, 1926), pp. 9–20.

17. See, for example, T. Landré, *De Moderne Woninginrichting* (Amsterdam, 1914); C. de Lorm, *Het Gezellige Binnenhuis* (Rotterdam, 1927); W. Retera, *Ons Binnenhuis* (Amsterdam, n.d.); J. L. M. Lauweriks, *Nieuwe Nederlandsche Ruimte-Kunst* (Blaricum, 1927).

18. See T. Landré, op. cit. (note 12).

19. C. de Lorm, op. cit. (note 12), pp. 3–4.

20. Most data are gathered from books and journals of their times, specifically from *Wendingen*. Many pieces of furniture, as well as sketches and drafts, are lost. De Klerk's and Kramer's archives are kept in the Nederlands Documentatiecentrum voor de Bouwkunst (Netherlands Center for Documentation of Architecture) in Amsterdam.

21. These sketches were published posthumously in *Wendingen* 6, no. 2 (1924).

22. Frans van Burkom alerted me to the claws attached to the closing mechanism of a combination print cabinet/bookcase designed by De Klerk; it appears that the user might injure his hands on them.

23. The correctness of these associations has not yet been explored. But from a drawing (Collection NDB) for a design of a pear-shaped clock on pointed feet slanted upward we may conclude that De Klerk himself thought of shoes in such a design. He stressed the anthropomorphic aspects by sketching eyes and a nose in the drawing (in the realized object they are absent). In this way, we can see the dial as a mouth.

24. H. Th. Wijdeveld, "Beschouwingen over M. de Klerk," *Wendingen* 7, no. 10 (1925), p. 3.

25. W. Retera, *P. Kramer* (Amsterdam, n.d.), p. 39.

26. Michel de Klerk, "Driebondgedachte en gedachten," *Architectura* 25, nos. 39–40 (1917), p. 20.

27. The exhibition was organized through the initiative of the Amsterdamsche Coöperatieve Vereeniging "Samenwerking" (Amsterdam Cooperative Society "Cooperation"). See *80 jaar wonen in het Stedelijk*, exhibition catalogue (Amsterdam: Stedelijk Museum, 1981), pp. 8–9.

28. J. M. van der Mey, "De arbeid van den Driebond in verband met het meubel," *Architectura* 25, nos. 39–40 (1917), p. 10.

29. H. Hana, *Ornamentontwerpen voor Iedereen: Het Stempelboekje* (Amsterdam, 1914), p. 7.

Karin Gaillard

THE AMSTERDAM SCHOOL AND PUBLIC HOUSING: HOUSING POLICY IN THE NETHERLANDS BETWEEN 1850 AND 1925

T HE design of workers' dwellings figured importantly in the activities of the Amsterdam School architects. A concerted effort to provide sorely needed public housing brought them numerous commissions. This effort was the culmination of decades of growing concern. Although Amsterdam had suffered a great shortage of workers' dwellings from the middle of the nineteenth century on, it was not until the beginning of the twentieth century—after several reports had been written and small-scale attempts were made to alleviate it—that the problem was tackled on a large scale. This development grew from many different political and socio-economic factors.[1]

With the rise of industry and the general agricultural depression in the second half of the nineteenth century, an ever increasing number of people left the countryside for the large centers of commerce and industry. The population of Amsterdam, where economic activities were growing rapidly, skyrocketed: between 1873 and 1901, the number of inhabitants rose from 221,165 to more than 500,000.[2]

This established a new urban proletariat, which could scarcely be accommodated. Speculators quickly took advantage of the situation: they subdivided old premises into small rooms, for which they charged exorbitant rents; they built up courtyards in old city quarters; they hastily erected many shoddy back-to-back dwellings. Most of these consisted of one room with an adjoining sleeping alcove, a kitchen or pantry, and a toilet. The speculators

Opposite: *Basement dwellings on Zeedijk no. 58, Amsterdam. From* Amsterdamse Woningraad. De Verbetering der Volkshuisvesting in Amsterdam *(Amsterdam, 1913)*

Houses in Joden Houttuinen, Amsterdam. From Amsterdamse Woningraad. De Verbetering der Volkshuisvesting in Amsterdam *(Amsterdam, 1913)*

built them as cheaply as possible and demanded as high a price as the market would bear.

This housing was beyond the means of most low-income workers, who lived in even worse quarters: dark, stuffy attics or damp basements, often without a toilet, water supply, plumbing, or sewers. Not surprisingly, many fearful diseases and epidemics broke out in these places. One result was that infant mortality rates in these basement dwellings were much higher than in other city dwellings.[3]

As early as the middle of the nineteenth century, all kinds of publications about the housing problem, following English examples, appeared in the Netherlands. In 1853, King William III commissioned the Royal Institute of Engineers to do a study on "the requirements and spatial arrangement of workers' dwellings" that would be sanitary as well as inexpensive. The research report, which appeared in 1855, vividly described the wretched living conditions of the working class. According to the report, many workers' dwellings, not much better than animal caves, were the sources of illnesses "spreading widely, so that they affect all classes, and are a scourge of destruction, also in the houses of the more cultured citizens."[4]

In spite of the report's plea and the concrete propositions made in this as well as in other publications to achieve improvement of public housing, in practice virtually nothing was done. Under the sway of the liberal "laisser faire, laisser aller" policy of the central government and the municipalities, government authorities, with few exceptions, held aloof from the problem. This attitude did not change until the beginning of the twentieth century.[5]

Several institutions concerned with the improvement of public housing attempted to fill the gap left by the government in the second half of the nineteenth century. These were a few semiphilanthropic housing associations and corporations founded by workers themselves. Well-meaning affluent citizens such as bankers and merchants, motivated by their enlightened ideal of "uplifting the working class" as well as by their own interests, were the mainstay of the former. Through the construction of good, sanitary dwellings, they hoped to combat alcoholism among the workers, to promote domesticity among the inhabitants, and, at the same time, to curb epidemics, which also threatened the higher classes. They realized that, in the long run, sanitary dwellings would influence positively the workers' productivity: "We are coming to understand that, like the machine, the worker needs good quarters in order to be productive."[6] Although these associations were partly profitable, profits were generally small. Examples of this kind in Amsterdam were De Vereeniging ten behoeve der Arbeiders-klasse (Association for the Benefit of the Working Class), founded in 1852, Salerno (1854), and the construction firm Concordia (1865).

With the rise of the labor movement in the Netherlands around 1870, workers' construction societies came into existence. The first in Amsterdam, founded in 1868, was the Bouwmaatschappij tot Verkrijging van Eigen Woningen (Construction Firm for the Acquisition of Private Dwellings).[7] It originally aimed to provide "a freestanding house with a small yard for every worker's family,"[8] which the inhabitants could gradually acquire by means of a savings system on the basis of their rent. When this proved impractical, the society instead built apartment blocks, the apartments being rented to its members by lottery.

These societies continued the use of the "back-to-back" system, and one-room apartments with bedsteads or sleeping alcoves were still fairly common. In general, however, their dwellings were somewhat better than those built by speculators. They had toilets, cold running water, and sewers, among other things, and care was taken that sufficient fresh air could enter. Some societies, in order to avoid the possibility of incest, called for separate bedrooms for children of the opposite sex. It should be noted, however, that there were only a very small number of such units, "some islands in the sea of slums," as the historian I. J. Brugmans stated.[9] Moreover, even these were still too expensive for most workers.

It was not until the government stepped in with the introduction of the Housing Act in 1902—the first real governmental action in the field of housing—that the situation actually improved. The Housing Act required every municipality in the Netherlands to formulate a building code. It regulated condemnation procedures, eviction, demolition, and expropriation of dwellings. Also, it enabled municipalities and associations for the benefit of public housing to receive financial aid from the central government.[10] Later, a system of premiums for private construction was established.

Most of the Housing Act's regulations had already been advocated in earlier publications. The report drawn up in 1896 under the auspices of the Maatschappij tot Nut van 't Algemeen (Public Benefit Society), entitled "The Problem of Public Housing," undoubtedly influenced the passage of the Housing Act.

The first building code of Amsterdam dates from 1905.[11] It was drafted by J. W. C. Tellegen, director of the municipal Department of Supervision on Construction and Housing, and later mayor of Amsterdam (1915–21). The code contained regulations pertaining to lot lines, foundations, and roofing, as well as the size of rooms, illumination, ventilation, and so on.

Article 139 of this code required that every dwelling in Amsterdam consist of at least an entrance hall, one or two rooms of at least forty cubic meters (about 1,400 cubic feet), one of which should be connected to a smoke vent, a toilet, and a pantry or a separate kitchen with a sink. Alcoves were prohibited.[12] The living area was to be at least

twenty-five square meters (about 270 square feet).[13] Air ducts and movable windows, the area of which had to be at least one-twentieth of the wall surface of the room, were also required.[14]

With the possibility of receiving financial aid from the government, in the form of loans or subsidies, many new construction societies sprang up. By 1923, no less than fifty-seven of these were active in Amsterdam.[15] The Rochdale Association built the first apartment block in Amsterdam realized in accordance with the Housing Act. Located in Van Beuningen Street, it was finished in 1909. Each dwelling consisted of a corridor, a living room, two separate bedrooms, a kitchen, a toilet, and a balcony. Uncharacteristically for those times, the interior as well as the exterior was designed by an architect, J. E. van der Pek (1865–1919). In the nineteenth century particularly, and even into the twentieth, often only the facades of inexpensive public housing projects were designed by an architect, while the floor plans usually were drawn up by the builder himself, a much less costly procedure. Although mostly private construction firms took advantage of this system, it was also regularly used by societies.

The National Housing Council, founded in 1913 as an umbrella for a large number of Dutch housing societies, from 1918 repeatedly urged its members to call in a "capable architect" for the design and execution of new buildings instead of leaving this to the "local carpenter." The latter usually

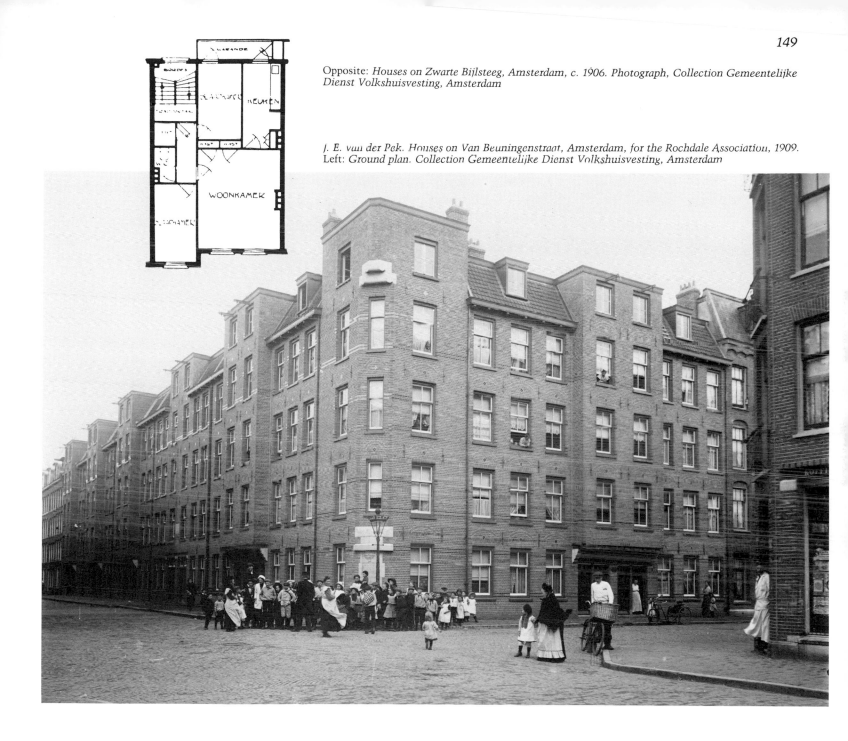

Opposite: *Houses on Zwarte Bijlsteeg, Amsterdam, c. 1906. Photograph, Collection Gemeentelijke Dienst Volkshuisvesting, Amsterdam*

J. E. van der Pek. Houses on Van Beuningenstraat, Amsterdam, for the Rochdale Association, 1909. Left: Ground plan. Collection Gemeentelijke Dienst Volkshuisvesting, Amsterdam

modeled his building on existing examples, from which he took bad elements along with the good. An architect, it was assumed, would avoid the undesirable elements and was, better than anyone else, capable of determining how a successful subdivision—successful in an aesthetic as well as a practical sense—should look.[16]

In the period between 1915 and 1930, Amsterdam saw a great deal of building activity.[17] Apart from the societies and private construction firms, the city also entered the arena as a commissioning agency.

An important factor behind this action was the Social-Democratic Labor Party (SDAP). In 1903, the first time that the SDAP had been represented in the City Council, it held only one seat out of forty-five, but eight years later it already held twelve seats.[18] The appointment of SDAP member F. M. Wibaut (1859–1936) as Alderman for Public Housing (1914) marked the beginning of a long period of Social-Democratic policy in this field.

In order to deal with the great housing need of that moment,[19] the SDAP councilors in 1911 submitted a proposal for the construction of two thousand dwellings to be commissioned by the city. These dwellings, destined for workers with the lowest incomes, would have to be rented at rates (1.80 to 2.50 guilders per week) that did not cover the costs. Tellegen, in his capacity as head of the municipal Department of Supervision on Construction and Housing, was asked to submit his com-

ments on this plan. His report came out three years later, by which time, he found, not two thousand but thirty-five hundred new workers' dwellings were needed. In addition, eight hundred dwellings would have to go up every year until 1922 in order to prevent a new emergency. In 1915, the City Council adopted this proposal, and construction soon began.[20]

To implement and manage these new dwellings, the council created a separate Housing Authority and named A. Keppler (1867–1941) its head. In addition to the tasks mentioned above, it was charged with the supervision of the housing societies. In 1925, it managed about 10 percent of all dwellings in Amsterdam; 6,986 of these were city-owned, and 11,561 had been built by the housing societies.[21]

Because of the First World War, the Housing Authority did not get off to a smooth start. High construction costs and the scarcity of materials impeded construction by the societies, and private construction almost completely stagnated. The housing shortage rapidly grew worse. As the problem became more urgent, thoughts gravitated toward the construction of temporary dwellings as an immediate solution. Although Wibaut as well as Keppler initially voiced strong opposition, the city went ahead with the plan in 1917. Within a period of four and a half months, 306 temporary dwellings were realized; they were demolished as late as 1929.[22]

The city also tackled the problem of

Opposite, above: *Zeeburgerdorp (municipal housing for asocial families), Amsterdam.* From De huisvesting van Asociale gezinnen te Amsterdam *(Amsterdam, 1929)*

Opposite, below: *H. van Dorp. Interior designed for workers, "Exhibition for Interior Design," Stedelijk Museum, Amsterdam, 1921. Collection NDB, Amsterdam*

housing for asocial families. "It is impossible to admit them into the blocks for normal families, because they would by their behavior interfere with the desired order, hygiene, and peace in these blocks."[23] Two remote dwelling complexes—Aster Village and Zeeburger Village (1925–26)—were built for those families. Here, under the guidance of a female supervisor who was specifically trained for this task at the School of Social Work in Amsterdam, they were taught "the elementary principles of good living."[24]

Following English examples,[25] female supervisors were appointed for the other blocks of city dwellings, too, as well as for those of many societies. It was their job to collect rents and oversee the correct use and maintenance of the premises. By cultivating intimate and confidential relations with the housewives, they sought to teach them the necessity of hygiene, advised them on child rearing, and so on. They also sometimes organized recreational outings for the inhabitants.

It is uncertain whether advice about furnishing the dwellings was among the cultural tasks of the supervisors.[26] It is clear, though, that several housing societies themselves, and such organizations as the National Housing Council, took the initiative to improve the workers' interiors. Thus, in a few new blocks, model dwellings were furnished with sober, simple furniture, and lectures were held about the "responsible" worker's interior. In 1921, the Amsterdamsche Coöperatieve Ver-

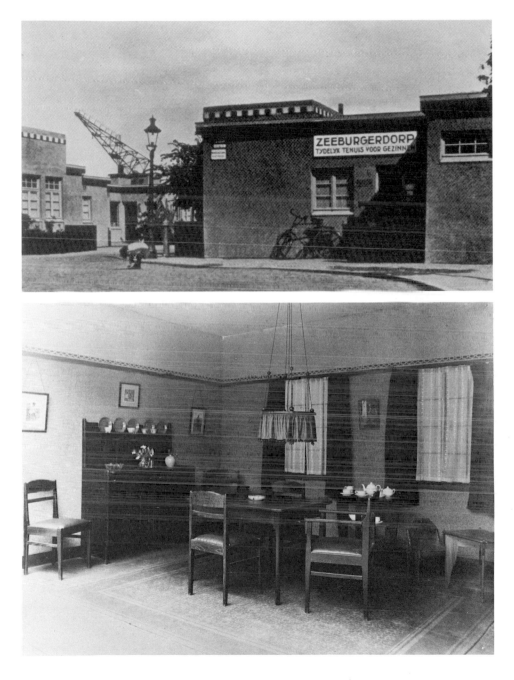

eeniging "Samenwerking" (Amsterdam Cooperative Society "Cooperation") sponsored a large exhibition of interior decoration in the Stedelijk Museum, Amsterdam. People like Wibaut and Keppler, who believed that not only a good dwelling but also a good interior could contribute to the well-being and happiness of the workers, played prominent roles in organizing this exhibition. Keppler particularly devoted himself to this aspect of public housing. Notwithstanding the large number of visitors, it is safe to assume that the influence of this exhibition on the workers was minimal.

The interiors exhibited were designed by well-known architects and furniture designers. The idea was that, if there was sufficient interest, the furniture would be mass-produced so that workers also could afford it. Unfortunately, this did not work out in practice. In any case, the workers did not find these interiors to their taste. The average workman owned excessively decorated furniture, executed in "neo" styles, which he had bought cheaply at department stores and bazaars. Contrary to the expectations of the interior reformers, the workers' "bad taste" did not change simply through being consistently confronted with "responsible" furniture designs. Although it had many positive things to say of the exhibition in the Stedelijk Museum, the press also expressed some criticism, particularly about its patronizing character.[27]

Another idea for the construction of new public housing that was adopted in the Netherlands, albeit with some modifications, was the garden city movement, which originated in England at the end of the nineteenth century. The idea of the garden city, initially envisioned as a utopian community, responded to uneasiness concerning the miserable living conditions of the workers in the overpopulated English cities due to industrialization. Ebenezer Howard (1850–1928), in his book *Garden Cities of To-Morrow*, described the ideal Garden City: a city built on a human scale, filled with greenery (gardens and parks), and surrounded by estates; it would be economically autonomous, with its own agriculture and industries.[28] Such an autonomous garden city has never been realized in the Netherlands. The *tuindorpen* ("garden villages") that originated here were in reality only spaciously built new city quarters, exclusively residential. Well-known garden villages include Vreewijk in Rotterdam (1916–19) and Oog in Al in Utrecht (from 1920 on).

In Amsterdam, too, where Keppler was among the followers of the garden city movement, some garden villages came into being in the twenties, including Tuindorp Oostzaan, Tuindorp Nieuwendam (1927), and Tuindorp Buiksloterham (1928–29), all of them situated in the northern section of Amsterdam.[29] These garden villages, rather geometric in layout, are primarily made up of one-family houses constructed in light materials. Tuindorp Watergraafsmeer (1923–28)—which later became known as Betondorp (Concrete Village)—was the first full-scale experiment with construction systems in concrete. Whereas most of the buildings in these garden-village projects were low-rise (although Betondorp also had duplexes), the other new building projects in Amsterdam were mainly executed as apartment buildings of three or four floors.

The boom in public housing construction in the beginning of the twenties coincided with the heyday of the Amsterdam School, which became deeply involved in this field. Many of the building complexes mentioned here were designed by exponents of this movement.

The fact that they received the largest number of commissions has been explained by the influence of the Schoonheidscommissie (Committee for Aesthetic Advice) on the new building projects. This committee of six architects (plus six substitutes), among other things, advised on and made decisions about new facade designs for buildings on city-owned land held on long-term leases by the housing societies. These facades had to harmonize in design with the existing buildings in the neighborhood.[30] In the twenties, most of the members of the Schoonheidscommissie were architects belonging to the Amsterdam School.[31] This circumstance undoubtedly affected the decisions that emerged from the committee.

Moreover, the City Council as well as

J. H. Mulder, Jr. Housing in the garden village Nieuwendam, on Volendammerweg, Amsterdam, 1928–29. Photograph, Collection Gemeentelijke Dienst Volkshuisvesting, Amsterdam

Right: *J. Gratama. Housing block in the Stadionbuurt, Amsterdam, 1925. View through a gate on Olympiakade toward an inner street. Photograph by Thérèse Bonney, Collection Cooper-Hewitt Museum, New York*

Below: *D. Greiner. Clubhouse on Brink, Betondorp, Amsterdam, 1922–26*

Michel de Klerk. Third block (left) and first block (right) on the Spaarndammerplantsoen. Photograph by Thérèse Bonney, Collection Cooper-Hewitt Museum, New York

several municipal departments concerned with public housing had exponents of the Amsterdam School or kindred spirits in their ranks.[32] Finally, it is possible that the National Housing Council, which encouraged housing societies to engage capable architects for new public housing projects, may also have promoted commissions to architects of the Amsterdam School. In September 1918, it sent its first list of "capable architects" to all its members. This list contained a significant number of architects working in the style of the Amsterdam School or akin to it.[33]

Among the housing societies that awarded commissions to Amsterdam School architects were Eigen Haard (Our Hearth), De Dageraad (The Dawn), and the earlier mentioned "Samenwerking."

Because of favorable social and economic circumstances—namely, the prevalent conception of good housing as a means of elevating working-class people to a higher social level and the fact that during and just after the First World War public housing was almost the only source of building commissions—architects of the Amsterdam School automatically became involved with public housing. After recognizing the construction of public housing as a valuable outlet, the Amsterdam School made use of its connection with the Schoonheidscommissie in order to mold the look of modern Amsterdam, just emerging after the war, to its vision.

Above: *W. Greve. Concrete housing in Betondorp, Amsterdam, 1923-25. Photograph, Collection Gemeentelijke Dienst Volkshuisvesting, Amsterdam*

Below: *J. B. van Loghem and W. Greve. Concrete housing in Betondorp, Amsterdam, 1922-25. Photograph, Collection Gemeentelijke Dienst Volkshuisvesting, Amsterdam*

Piet Kramer. Housing block in Amsterdam-South. Photograph by Thérèse Bonney, Collection Cooper-Hewitt Museum, New York

J. F. Staal. Housing block on J. M. Coenenstraat and Bartholomeus Ruloffstraat, Amsterdam, for "Samenwerking," 1922–23. Perspective, watercolor and ink. Collection NDB, Amsterdam

NOTES

1. Publications dealing in greater depth with this topic: Ellinoor Bergvelt, "Wetgeving en sociaal-economische achtergronden," in *Nederlandse architectuur 1910-1930, Amsterdamse School* (Amsterdam: Stedelijk Museum, 1975), pp. 15-33; Egbert Ottens, *Ik moet naar een kleinere woning omzien want mijn gezin wordt te groot* (Amsterdam: Gemeentelijke Dienst Volkshuisvesting, 1975); Carol Schade, *Woningbouw voor arbeiders in het 19de-eeuwse Amsterdam* (Amsterdam: Van Gennep, 1981).

2. Frank Smit, "Gemeente als vliegwiel voor volkshuisvesting," Wonen-TA/BK, no. 14 (1973), p. 20.

3. *De Verbetering der Volkshuisvesting te Amsterdam* (Amsterdam, 1913), p. 33.

4. *Verslag aan den Koning over de vereischten en inrigting van arbeiderswoningen* (Report of the Royal Institute of Engineers), 1855, p. 4.

5. In 1875 the City of Amsterdam loaned 1,800,000 guilders to the Amsterdam Society for the construction of workers' dwellings at a low interest rate. Moreover, it made building sites available for free. Egbert Ottens, op. cit. (note 1), pp. 9-10.

6. D. O. Engelen, *Over Arbeiderswoningen* (Utrecht, 1870).

7. The first board of directors consisted primarily of workers, but later, the employers tended to dominate.

8. "Honderd jaar wonen," in *Jaarverslag Bouwmaatschappij tot Verkrijging van Eigen Woningen* (Amsterdam, 1968), p. 20.

9. I. J. Brugmans, *De Arbeidende Klasse in Nederland in de 19e eeuw*, (Utrecht, 1971; 1st ed. 1925), p. 160.

10. The amount of government aid changed every year. The largest advances and subsidies were granted in times of economic recession. When there was a boom, the financial aid was reduced; in 1923 it was abolished altogether.

11. Amsterdam had some earlier building codes for dwellings, but these were very summary. They were primarily aimed at reducing fire hazards (construction of wooden houses was prohibited). There were no regulations about interiors.

12. *Amsterdamse Bouwverordening 1905*, Article 146.

13. Ibid., Article 138. Walls, corridors, staircases, and attics were not included in this area.

14. Ibid., Article 146.

15. Frank Smit, op. cit. (note 2), p. 26.

16. From a communication, dated September 1918, by the National Housing Societies to all housing associations, published in *Woningbouw*, no. 3 (1918), pp. 5–7.

17. In 1921, 3,178 dwellings were built in Amsterdam. For the years 1922 through 1925, the numbers were, respectively: 6,384; 5,216; 7,282; and 8,402. From P. Hoogland, *Vijf en twintig jaren Sociaal-Democratie in de Hoofdstad* (Amsterdam, 1928), p. 169. Cited in Adriaan Venema, "Sociaal-economische aspecten van de Amsterdamse School," in *Nederlandse architectuur 1910–1930, Amsterdamse School* (Amsterdam: Stedelijk Museum, 1975), p. 7.

18. Adriaan Venema, op. cit. (note 17), p. 5.

19. In 1915, Amsterdam had a housing shortage of 5,154 dwellings. A. Keppler, *Bij het tienjarig bestaan van den Gemeentelijken Woningdienst te Amsterdam* (Amsterdam, 1925). Cited in Egbert Ottens, op. cit. (note 1), p. 77.

20. Egbert Ottens, op. cit. (note 1), pp. 26–27.

21. Ibid., p. 78.

22. Ibid., p. 34. Later, more of these temporary dwellings were built by the city.

23. *Huisvesting van a-sociale gezinnen te Amsterdam* (Amsterdam: Gemeentelijke Woningdienst, 1929). Cited in Frank Smit, op. cit. (note 2), p. 22.

24. Description by Keppler. Egbert Ottens, op. cit. (note 1), p. 88.

25. Octavia Hill (1838–1912) was the first housing supervisor. She trained several of the first Dutch supervisors, including Johanna ter Meulen and Louise Went. The training program at the School of Social Work was initiated in 1899.

26. Ali de Regt, who has done research about the activities of the dwelling supervisors, says nothing about this. Ali de Regt, "Woningopzichteressen: een mislukt professionaliseringsproces," *Amsterdams Sociologisch Tijdschrift* 6 (1979), pp. 418–48.

27. See, for example, J. P. Mieras, "Amsterdamsche Tentoonstelling van Woninginrichting in het Stedelijk Museum," *Bouwkundig Weekblad* 42 (1921), pp. 161–63.

28. Ebenezer Howard, *Garden Cities of To-Morrow* (London: Sonnenschein, 1902).

29. Several of these, like Oostzaan and Nieuwendam, were annexed by Amsterdam in 1921.

30. Note that judgment by the Schoonheidscommissie was only required for the facades! As mentioned earlier, this resulted in the practice that developers, especially those in private enterprise, had the facades designed by architects but did the floor plans themselves.

31. Wim de Wit, "De Amsterdamse School" (*doctoraal* thesis, Nijmegen, 1973), p. 65. Cited in Adriaan Venema, op. cit. (note 17), p. 9.

32. For instance, the architect A. R. Hulshoff was at that time director of the buildings section of the Municipal Department for Buildings and Works. Cf. Richter Roegholt, *Amsterdam in de 20e eeuw*, vol. 1 (Utrecht: Spectrum, 1976), p. 32.

33. These included B. T. Boeyinga, P. L. Kramer, J. F. Staal, and H. Th. Wijdeveld. Michel de Klerk was a member of the committee that compiled the list of architects. Cf. further note 2.

BIBLIOGRAPHY

Canella, G. "L'Epopea borghese della Scuola di Amsterdam." *Casabella*, no. 215 (1957), pp. 76–91.

Casciato, Maristella; Panzini, Franco; and Polano, Sergio. *Funzione e Senso, Architettura Casa Città, Olanda 1870–1940*. Milan: Gruppo Editoriale Electa, 1979. Dutch edition: *Architektuur en Volkshuisvesting Nederland 1870–1940*. Nijmegen: Socialistiese Vitgeverij, 1980.

Casciato, Maristella, and De Wit, Wim. *Lo Eigen Haard di Michel de Klerk 1913–1921*. Rome: Officina, 1983.

Fanelli, Giovanni. *Architettura Moderna in Olanda 1900–1940*. Florence: Marchi e Bertolli, 1968. Dutch revised edition: *Moderne architectuur in Nederland 1900–1940*. The Hague: Staatsuitgeverij, 1978. Gives an extensive bibliography about Dutch architecture up to 1978.

Fanelli, Giovanni. *Architettura, Edilizia, Urbanistica Olanda 1917–1940*. Florence: F. Papafava, 1978.

Fanelli, Giovanni, and Godoli, Ezio, eds. *Wendingen 1918–1931, Documenti dell'arte olandese del Novecento*. Florence: Centro Di, 1982.

Fraenkel, Francis F. *Het Plan Amsterdam-Zuid van H. P. Berlage*. Alphen aan de Rijn: Samson's Uitgeverij, 1976.

Frank, Suzanne S. "Michel de Klerk (1884–1923): An Architect of the Amsterdam School." Ph.D. dissertation, Columbia University, 1969.

Frank, Suzanne S. "Michel de Klerk's Design for Amsterdam Spaarndammerbuurt 1914–1920." In *Nederlands Kunsthistorisch Jaarboek* 22 (1971), pp. 175–213.

Nederlandse architectuur 1910–1930, Amsterdamse School, Amsterdam: Stedelijk Museum, 1975.

Nycolaas, Jacques. *Volkshuisvesting, een bijdrage tot de geschiedenis van woningbouw en woningbouwbeleid*. Nijmegen: Socialistiese Uitgeverij, 1974.

Ottens, Egbert. *Ik moet naar een kleinere woning omzien want mijn gezin wordt te groot*. Amsterdam: Gemeentelijke Dienst Volkshuisvesting, 1975.

Pehnt, Wolfgang. *Expressionist Architecture*. London: Thames and Hudson, 1973.

Pennink, P. K. A. "Betondorp." *Forum*, no. 4 (1965).

Searing, Helen. "Housing in Holland and the Amsterdam School." Ph.D. dissertation, Yale University, 1971.

Searing, Helen. "'Eigen Haard': Workers Housing and the Amsterdam School." *Architectura* 1, no. 2 (1971), pp. 148–75.

Searing, Helen. "With Red Flags Flying: Housing in Amsterdam, 1915–1923." In *Art and Architecture in the Service of Politics*, ed. Henri A. Millon and Linda Nochlin. Cambridge, Mass.: The MIT Press, 1978.

Searing, Helen. "Amsterdam South: Social Democracy's Elusive Housing Ideal," *Culture and the Social Vision, Via 4* (Architectural Journal of the Graduate School of Fine Arts, University of Pennsylvania). The MIT Press, 1980.

Searing, Helen. "Berlage or Cuypers? The Father of Them All." In *In Search of Modern Architecture: A Tribute to Henry-Russell Hitchcock*, ed. Helen Searing. New York: The Architectural History Foundation; Cambridge, Mass.: The MIT Press, 1982, pp. 226–44.

Sharp, Dennis. *Modern Architecture and Expressionism*. London: Longmans, 1966.

De Wit, Wim. "Die Amsterdamer Schule und die städtische Wohnbaupolitik." In *Kommunale Wohnbau in Wien, Aufbau 1923–1934 Ausstrahlung*, ed. Karl Mang. Vienna, 1977.

CHRONOLOGY

1898 Michel de Klerk begins to work at the architectural office of Eduard Cuypers, where he meets, among others, J. M. van der Mey, Piet L. Kramer, and G. F. la Croix.

1902 Housing Act enacted by Dutch parliament, allowing for state intervention in public housing.

1906 Michel de Klerk travels to London in an unsuccessful attempt to find work; thereafter he returns to Cuypers's office, where he remains until 1910.

1910 Michel de Klerk marries Lea Jessurun; he travels with her in Sweden and Denmark.

1911 Michel de Klerk starts his own architectural practice, as does Piet Kramer at about this time.

1912 Johan van der Mey is commissioned to build the Scheepvaarthuis, an office building for six shipping companies in Amsterdam. He invites De Klerk and Kramer to collaborate on the architectural design and also engages several decorative artists. The building is finished in 1916.

1913–15 De Klerk builds the first block at the Spaarndammerplantsoen in Amsterdam for the builder and contractor Klaas Hille.

1914–18 First World War; Holland remains neutral, but because of the war, building materials are difficult to obtain and become very expensive; during this period, private builders are not active in the construction of housing.

1914 F. M. Wibaut elected as the first socialist alderman in Amsterdam; he is responsible for public housing in Amsterdam until 1921.

1914–16 Second housing block at the Spaarndammerplantsoen built by De Klerk for the housing association Eigen Haard (Own Hearth).

1915 Establishment of the municipal Housing Authority in Amsterdam; A. Keppler is director until 1937. This department administers all housing built by the municipality.

1915 The Amsterdam Schoonheidscommissie (Committee for Aesthetic Advice) is reorganized, giving more power to architects to judge building designs on the basis of aesthetic criteria.

1917 Piet Kramer begins to work at the Municipal Department for Buildings and Works, where he designs more than four hundred bridges for the city of Amsterdam.

1917 Berlage's extension plan for Amsterdam-South accepted by the municipal council; a large part of this plan will be built by the architects of the Amsterdam School.

1917–18 A group of Amsterdam School architects builds sixteen country houses at Park Meerwijk in Bergen for A. Heystee. This project marks the first recognition of the Amsterdam School as a group.

1917–21 De Klerk builds a housing block on Zaanstraat, Oostzaanstraat, and Hembrugstraat (near the Spaarndammerplantsoen) in Amsterdam for the housing association Eigen Haard.

1918 The first housing blocks built in Amsterdam-South (on Amstelveenscheweg, Cornelis Krusemanstraat, and De Lairessestraat) by J. C. van Epen for the housing associations Rochdale and AWV (Algemeene Woningbouw Vereeniging).

1918 First issue of *Wendingen* published in January. H. Th. Wijdeveld is the editor.

1919–21 De Klerk and Kramer design and build a complex of housing blocks for the housing association De Dageraad (The Dawn) on Pieter Lodewijk Takstraat, Burgemeester Tellegenstraat, Henriette Ronnerplein, and Thérèse Schwartzeplein, Amsterdam.

1919–22 Amstels Bouw Vereeniging, a consortium of private builders-contractors, is the first private construction group to build housing blocks in Amsterdam South. In order to gain approval from the Schoonheidscommissie, they commission architects to design facades for blocks that the contractors designed themselves. Many Amsterdam School architects, including De Klerk, Kramer, Staal, Kropholler, La Croix, and Wijdeveld design a facade in this scheme.

1922–26 Construction of Betondorp, the first large-scale experiment in concrete housing in Amsterdam.

1923 Michel de Klerk dies on November 24, his thirty-ninth birthday.

1924–26 Five issues of *Wendingen* are devoted to De Klerk's work.

1925 Exposition Universelle des Arts décoratifs et industriels modernes in Paris. Dutch pavilion built by J. F. Staal. The fact that De Stijl was not represented constituted a triumph for the Amsterdam School.

1927 Reorganization of the editorial board of *Wendingen*; Wijdeveld retires from the magazine.

1931 After nos. 11–12 of volume 12, *Wendingen* ceases publication.

BIOGRAPHIES

Karel P. C. de Bazel (1869–1923)

While working in the office of the neo-Gothic architect P. J. H. Cuypers (1889–1895), De Bazel became friendly with J. L. M. Lauweriks, another Cuypers colleague. Together, they developed a design method on the basis of a geometrical system; this was to have an influence on many important Dutch architects, particularly Berlage. When in 1895 they were forced to leave Cuypers's office because of their theosophist sympathies, De Bazel and Lauweriks started an arts and crafts atelier for architecture, interior design, furniture, and graphic design. Lacking architectural commissions, De Bazel entered several competitions and otherwise specialized in furniture design. He also made woodcuts in which he expressed theosophist ideas symbolically.

After 1900, De Bazel started his own practice and became well known as an architect of country houses. In their ground plans he demonstrated an interest in English architecture.

De Bazel died in a train while he was on his way to De Klerk's funeral.

Hendrik P. Berlage (1856–1934)

Berlage is generally considered the most important innovator of twentieth-century Dutch architecture. In the Amsterdam Stock Exchange (1898–1903), he replaced historicizing references with a new style—a sober rationalism—in which external form was meant to be expressive of internal function and construction. This is evident in virtually all his buildings; protruding or receding volumes break through the surface of a facade to indicate spaces beyond. In order to preserve unity among the multiplicity of shapes he thus evolved, Berlage used a geometric system as a basis for the design of ground plans, elevations, and sections. Berlage was much impressed by the English Arts and Crafts movement, from which he adopted the practice of collaboration between architects, artists, and craftsmen, retaining all the while a predominant role for himself as master architect. His conception of architecture as the supreme art to which all others must submit was not always accepted by his collaborators.

Cornelis J. Blaauw (1885–1947)

In his early career (1917–25), Blaauw was one of the more important Amsterdam School architects. He built three country houses in Park Meerwijk in Bergen, a development in which J. F. Staal, M. Kropholler, Piet L. Kramer, and G. F. la Croix also built houses. The commission of these sixteen structures can be considered as the first recognition of the Amsterdam School as a group.

Blaauw contributed several articles to *Wendingen*, in which he advocated expressionist ideas that became characteristic of the Amsterdam School.

Blaauw's post-1925 work exemplifies the difficulties Amsterdam School architects encountered in designing interesting-looking housing blocks during a period of increasing standardization. He was unable to disguise the fact that his blocks were actually accumulations of identical dwellings while, on

Left: *H. P. Berlage*; right: *K. P. C. de Bazel*

the other hand, his expressionist proclivities prevented him from making a positive statement in rationalistic terms.

Jan Boterenbrood (1886–1932)

Boterenbrood became one of the so-called second-generation Amsterdam School architects when his work began to be influenced by the style of the original group (e.g., De Klerk, Kramer, Staal, Wijdeveld). However, he remained untouched by the expressionist ideology, which involved a conjunction of individualism and utopian universalism. This fact may explain a certain lack of fantasy in his work.

Guillaume F. la Croix (1877–1923)

From the moment that La Croix and De Klerk met in Eduard Cuypers's office, they became close friends. They must have recognized in each other a shared sensitivity and unworldly character. Unlike De Klerk, La Croix could not overcome his instinctual reserve with patrons. He therefore received few commissions in which he was able to demonstrate the high quality evident in his designs on paper.

Eduard Cuypers (1859–1927)

A nephew of the neo-Gothic architect P. J. H. Cuypers, who taught him architectural design, Eduard established his own practice in 1878. After having worked for some years in a neo-Renaissance style, around 1900 he came under the influence of the Arts and Crafts movement and changed his office into an atelier for architecture and interior design, modeled on the workshops of Morris and other English designers. In 1904 he started the publication of a magazine, *Het Huis*, in which he displayed his own work exclusively. During this period, Cuypers had many young assistants working as draftsmen in his office, several of whom, including De Klerk, Kramer, Van der Mey, and La Croix, were later to become leading architects of the Amsterdam School.

A. Eibink (1893–1975) and J. A. Snellebrand (1891–1963)

Between 1915 and 1924, Eibink and Snellebrand made a number of very striking designs that clearly show their interest in organic architecture. For such an architecture, they considered concrete to be the most appropriate material, and they were very innovative in their ideas about its use. Most people judged designs such as the church in Elshout as too peculiar, and it therefore remained unrealized, like many other of their most advanced designs.

Job C. van Epen (1880–1960)

A specialist in the building of housing blocks, Van Epen always showed great concern for good ground plans. His abundant use of bay windows proceeded from his wish to ensure that there would be enough light in the dwelling; at the same time, bay windows—as well as buttresses and the color of the woodwork—were meant to enliven the facade.

Jan Gratama (1877–1947)

Having begun his career as an admirer and follower of Berlage's rationalism, after 1915 Gratama applied more decoration to his architecture. In his concrete buildings especially, he developed a coloristic and sometimes floral decoration in order to brighten the grayness of the material. Apart from these experiments, Gratama is known for his publications and for the official positions he occupied in architectural organizations rather than for the distinctiveness of his oeuvre.

Dick Greiner (1891–1964)

The most famous works Greiner created are the housing blocks, a library, and a communal house in Betondorp (1922–26), a sort of garden city in Amsterdam that, as an experiment in cheap housing, was built almost entirely in concrete. Because of his use here of prefabricated wall elements, Greiner could not apply voluminous Amsterdam School forms as he did in other buildings. He nonetheless managed to deploy the concrete slabs in a decorative manner; to enliven them further, he employed colored tiles. Even the window divisions were carefully calculated for their aesthetic effect on the whole.

Michel de Klerk (1884–1923)

De Klerk was without any doubt the most important architect of the Amsterdam School. He began his career very early (1898) in the office of Eduard Cuypers. He remained there until 1910, with only a short interruption for a trip to England, where he tried unsuccessfully to find a job in 1906. His first commission was a middle-class housing block on the Johannes Vermeerplein in Amsterdam for the builder and contractor Klaas Hille, who later commissioned him to build the first block at the Spaarndammerplantsoen complex. This complex, three working-class housing blocks built for Hille and the housing association Eigen Haard between 1913 and 1921, demonstrates a continuation of the nascent expressionist style of the Scheepvaarthuis (by Van der Mey, De Klerk, and Kramer, 1912–16) and at the same time marks the high point of achievement by De Klerk and the Amsterdam School. De Dageraad (The Dawn), a housing complex for the socialist diamond workers housing association of the same name, was designed and built in collaboration with Piet Kramer between 1919 and 1921. It is especially interesting because of its decorative details and craftsmanship, but lacks the organic vitality of the third block on the Spaarndammerplantsoen (1917–21). Although De Klerk always refused to act as a leader, it is clear that his architect colleagues considered him as such. After his untimely death on his thirty-ninth birthday in 1923, five issues of *Wendingen* were devoted to his work.

Piet L. Kramer (1881–1961)

Between 1917 and 1952, Kramer worked as architect at the Municipal Department for Buildings and Works in Amsterdam. In this capacity he was given an opportunity to design more than four hundred bridges that had to be built because of increasing automobile traffic. Many of his structures involve the use of brick and stone to mask a steel supporting structure.

In addition to this work, Kramer also designed country houses and housing blocks, the most famous of which is the Dageraad complex that he designed and built together with Michel de Klerk between 1919 and 1921.

In 1925, he participated in the competition for the Bijenkorf department store in The Hague. Although not the

winner, he was nonetheless given the commission; J. F. Staal's design, which was actually chosen by the jury, was considered too advanced by the patron. Kramer's Bijenkorf can be regarded as the last original Amsterdam School creation. Thereafter, the group's style was increasingly reduced to the repetition of the same formal elements.

Willem Kromhout (1864–1940)

Kromhout's career consists of two seemingly opposed elements. On the one hand, throughout his life he showed a great concern for improving architectural education and revaluing the profession of the architect in general. On the other hand, he was interested in visionary design and had a highly artistic concept of architectural practice. Kromhout believed that once the schooling and economic situation of architects were better organized, every architect would be an artist.

Hildo Krop (1884–1970)

Originally trained as a pastry chef, Krop took up sculpture professionally around 1910. His first major project was the decoration of the Scheepvaarthuis (1912–16), on which he worked in collaboration with the more experienced sculptor H. A. van der Eijnde. In 1916 Krop was appointed sculptor of the City of Amsterdam. This position—which Krop held until his death—attests to the importance Amsterdam attached to sculpture in the urban environment. In this capacity, Krop made numerous sculptures for bridges designed by Piet Kramer as well as for housing blocks designed by other Amsterdam School architects. At the same time, he was also active as a designer of furniture and decorative objects.

Margaret Kropholler (1891–1966)

During a relatively brief period between 1917 and 1925, Margaret Kropholler, the first female architect in the Netherlands, designed some very interesting Amsterdam School buildings. Of these, three country houses in Park Meerwijk in Bergen are the most important. During the thirties, Kropholler designed few buildings, but after the Second World War she resumed her architectural practice and was involved in the reconstruction of cities damaged by the war.

J. L. Mathieu Lauweriks (1864–1932)

Even more than De Bazel, Lauweriks was a fiery defender of design methods based on geometric systems. A teacher by nature, his writings and lectures had a strong influence on architects both within and outside the Netherlands. While teaching at Peter Behrens's Kunstgewerbeschule in Dusseldorf (1904–9), Lauweriks's ideas had an impact on such young architects as Le Corbusier, Walter Gropius, and Adolf Meyer. From 1909 until 1916, Lauweriks taught and worked in Hagen for the banker and art patron K. E. Osthaus. Forced by the circumstances of the war to return to Holland in 1916, Lauweriks was appointed director of the Quellinus School in Amsterdam. In the following years he played an important role in the formation of the Amsterdam School ideology.

Johannes B. van Loghem (1881–1940)

Van Loghem's work reflects the close relationship of the many different architectural movements in the Netherlands during the first half of the twentieth century. Although he generally was more interested in rational ground plans than in expressionistic or organic forms, and only a few of his buildings (designed around 1918) show Amsterdam School characteristics, he was editor of *Wendingen* with only a few interruptions from the beginning of 1918 until 1926, when he went to Russia to build new cities in Siberia. After his return two years later, he became one of the leading architects of the Dutch functionalist movement.

Julius M. Luthmann (1890–1973)

From 1920 until 1923, Luthmann worked as architect for the State Department of Buildings and Works. The buildings he designed in this period for the radio station Kootwijk brought him international fame. These works are closely related to the architecture of both Peter Behrens and Erich Mendelsohn.

Johan M. van der Mey (1878–1949)

Having begun his career in the architectural office of Eduard Cuypers, Van der Mey soon developed into a promising architect. In 1906 he won the Prix de Rome, and two years later he won a competition for the reorganization of the Dam Square in Amsterdam. His most important architectural commission was the Scheepvaarthuis, also in Amsterdam (1912–16). For this structure he called upon the help of other architects (De Klerk and Kramer) as well as sculptors and decorative designers. The Scheepvaarthuis is generally considered to be the first building in the style that came to be associated with the Amsterdam School. It seems that after its completion, Van der Mey's creativity faded. The few housing blocks he accomplished lack almost entirely the freshness of the Scheepvaarthuis.

Richard N. Roland Holst (1869–1938)

In 1892, C. Veth published a Dutch translation of Walter Crane's *The Claims of Decorative Art*, which was widely read and immediately influential. Roland Holst's trip to England in 1893–94 was prompted by a desire to study Crane's work in its larger context. Roland Holst thus became the first Dutch artist to encounter William Morris. Upon his return to Holland, he was responsible for introducing others to Morris's oeuvre. The influence of the English Arts and Crafts movement is reflected in both Roland Holst's social-ist convictions and in the Symbolist stained-glass windows and the book designs that constitute his most important artistic work.

Frans E. Röntgen (1904–1982)

Röntgen built his most important building for his father, the composer Julius Röntgen. The villa, called Gaudeamus, was constructed in Bilthoven in 1925. A large portion of it is taken up by a round music room.

Jordanus Roodenburgh (1886–?)

In the beginning of the twenties, Roodenburgh became involved with housing blocks for private contractors who needed an architect in order to get their building plans accepted by the municipal Committee for Aesthetic Advice. Architects working in the private sector generally were not as free to spend money on decorative elements as were those who worked for housing associations or municipalities. Roodenburgh was unusual in his ability to achieve pleasing effects with a minimum of means.

J. Frits Staal (1879–1940)

Having at first been strongly influenced by Berlage's sober rationalism, after 1915 Staal admitted much more decoration into his designs and eventually became one of the leading architects of the Amsterdam School. It was he who received the commission for the Park Meerwijk development in Bergen; he designed its layout and chose four other architects to participate with him in building sixteen country houses there. After 1925, Staal once again returned to a less decorative idiom, in which he attempted to develop a style based on the play of volumes rather than adding decoration to the building.

Piet Vorkink (1878–1960) and Jacques Ph. Wormser (1878–1935)

During the period of their collaboration (from about 1905 until 1925), Vorkink and Wormser were principally involved with public housing. Their most important work, however, is the country house 't Reigersnest (The Heron's Nest) in Oostvoorne (1918–20), a characteristic example of organic architecture. Next to this structure they also built a gardener's house and a gazebo in the dunes. The latter, a small vaulted space that seemed to grow out of the dunes, was destroyed during the Second World War.

Hendrik Th. Wijdeveld (b. 1885)

The most exuberant of all the Amsterdam School architects, Wijdeveld is important not so much for what he built but for his international contacts with expressionist architects, including Mendelsohn, Taut, Finsterlin, and with the American Frank Lloyd Wright. Wijdeveld played a crucial role in propagating the ideas of the Amsterdam School through *Wendingen*, which he edited from 1918 until the end of 1926.

In his architecture he shows a great interest in utopian design.

PHOTO CREDITS

The editor and publishers wish to thank the museums and private individuals for permitting the reproduction of materials in their collections and for supplying the necessary photographs. Photographs from the following sources are gratefully acknowledged:

Courtesy Professor Robert Judson Clark, Princeton, N.J.: 77, 78(above), 78(below)

Cooper-Hewitt Museum, New York, Thérèse Bonney Collection: 154(above), 155, 157

Gemeentelijke Dienst Volkshuisvesting, Amsterdam: 148, 149, 153, 156(above), 156(below)

Nederlands Documentatiecentrum voor de Bouwkunst, Amsterdam: 10, 12, 32, 40, 42-43, 48-49, 166

Frank den Oudsten, Amsterdam: 11, 13, 14, 59(right), 63, 98, 102, 104, 106, 107(above, right), 107(below, right), 108, 110(left), 154(below)

Franco Panzini, Rome: 17, 18-19, 20, 21, 22, 23, 24-25, 26, 27, 28(left), 28(right), 94, 95, 96, 99, 100(left), 100(right), 101(left), 101(right), 103(left), 103(right), 105(left), 105(right), 107(left), 109, 110(right), 111(left), 111(right), 112, 113, 114-15, 116, 117, 118, 119

Rijksdienst voor de Monumentenzorg, Zeist (Ton Scholle, IJsbrand Heins, and Joop de Koning): 33, 34, 35, 36, 37, 44-45, 46, 52, 53, 55(above), 56, 58-59, 60, 61, 68, 69, 72, 74(right), 75, 76, 79(above), 79(below), 80(above), 80(below), 82, 83, 84(above), 84(below), 85, 87, 88, 90, 97, 130, 131(left), 131(right), 133(above), 133(below), 136, 164, 165(left), 166(right), 167

Helen Searing, Northampton, Mass.: 71, 73, 74(left), 81, 89

Stedelijk Museum, Amsterdam: 30, 31, 38-39, 41, 54, 55(below), 57, 62, 122, 123, 125, 126(above), 126(below), 127, 128, 129, 132, 134, 135, 137(above), 137(below), 139, 140, 141, 142, 143, 146, 147, 151(above), 151(below), 158-59, 165(right)

INDEX

Page numbers in **boldface** refer to illustrations